THE
GENIUS
OF
ONE

God's answer for our fractured world

GREG HOLDER

NAVPRESS®

A NavPress resource published in alliance
with Tyndale House Publishers, Inc.

NAVPRESS®.

NavPress is the publishing ministry of The Navigators, an international Christian organization and leader in personal spiritual development. NavPress is committed to helping people grow spiritually and enjoy lives of meaning and hope through personal and group resources that are biblically rooted, culturally relevant, and highly practical.

For more information, visit www.NavPress.com.

The Genius of One: God's Answer for Our Fractured World

Copyright © 2017 by Greg Holder. All rights reserved.

A NavPress resource published in alliance with Tyndale House Publishers, Inc.

NAVPRESS and the NAVPRESS logo are registered trademarks of NavPress, The Navigators, Colorado Springs, CO. *TYNDALE* is a registered trademark of Tyndale House Publishers, Inc. Absence of ® in connection with marks of NavPress or other parties does not indicate an absence of registration of those marks.

The Team:
Don Pape, Publisher
David Zimmerman, Acquisitions Editor
Caitlyn Carlson: Copyeditor
Mark Anthony Lane, Designer

Cover illustration of hand drawn by Mark Lane. Copyright © Tyndale House Publishers, Inc. All rights reserved.

Author photograph by Amee Rozanc, copyright © 2017. All rights reserved.

Published in association with the literary agency of Mark Sweeney & Associates.

Some of the anecdotal illustrations in this book are true to life and are included with the permission of the persons involved. All other illustrations are composites of real situations, and any resemblance to people living or dead is purely coincidental.

For information about special discounts for bulk purchases, please contact Tyndale House Publishers at csresponse@tyndale.com, or call 1-800-323-9400.

Cataloging-in-Publication Data is available.

ISBN 978-1-63146-631-1

Printed in the United States of America

23	22	21	20	19	18	17
7	6	5	4	3	2	1

Perhaps the one thing that most hinders the world-changing mission of the church is its lack of unity. Jesus prayed in John 17 that his church would be "one" so that the world would believe that God had sent him. In *The Genius of One*, you'll enjoy Greg's humor and his humility, but your greatest takeaway will be how your influence and leadership in embracing our oneness in Christ is the first step toward changing the world.

RICHARD STEARNS
President of World Vision US and author of *The Hole in Our Gospel*

Greg Holder is a trusted guide to lead you on a journey to discover God's heart for unity. His instructive encouragement is impeccable. In our divided culture, I can't imagine a more timely and critical message.

GABE LYONS
President of Q Ideas and author of *Good Faith* and *The Next Christians*

The Genius of One is a cynic buster. For more than forty years I have been involved in Kingdom matters, and I have suffered enough fools and my own foolishness to guffaw when I consider unity in the body of Christ. I love Greg and respect him enormously, but a book on what it means to be one in the church seemed as unlikely as seventy is the new fifty. His playful, hilarious, heartfelt, theologically profound invitation to risk humbly for unity is a clarion call in a world as fractured and toxic as ours. This compelling book will help you celebrate Jesus' call to reveal him by the way we relate.

DAN B. ALLENDER, PhD
Professor of counseling psychology at The Seattle School and author of *The Wounded Heart*

Greg Holder has written a clear and vivid piece on how we can actually attain peace through *The Genius of One*. This book not only envisions the possibilities of what we are called to be as one body; it also gives us colorful pictures and the practical nuts and bolts of how we can be the answer to Jesus' prayer of true oneness.

DR. DAVID A. ANDERSON
Author of *Gracism: The Art of Inclusion*

The Genius of One is a practitioner's handbook for how businesses, churches, and individuals can achieve more together than apart. Saturated with wisdom, humility, and lived experience, Holder offers one of the most gritty, earthy, and practical books on how believers can live out their common unity with God and one another in light of our many differences.

DAVE HICKMAN
Author of *Closer Than Close: Awakening to the Freedom of Your Union with Christ*

A rare book and a rare author. In teaching, who combines insight into Scripture that goes beyond commentary, a flair for the narrative, humor that's funny and not merely amusing, and illustrations that illuminate instead of reiterate? This guy—Greg Holder—that's who. *The Genius of One* is a profound unpacking of a profound thesis—everything worth anything in this world is rooted in the oneness of God. Do we know this? Did we know this and then forget? I'm not sure, but I've never seen it as clearly as I do now. Thanks, Greg. This book is a gem.

RICK JAMES
Publisher of CruPress and author of *Watch* and *A Million Ways to Die*

To Robin, Alexandra, and Victoria. From Caper
Wood to Mount Everest and every place in between,
the world is better when you are by my side.

BRENDA —
Hope you Enjoy
The Book !

JN17

CONTENTS

WHITE FOLDING CHAIRS

Why This Matters and What to Expect

WE HAVE FORGOTTEN HOW TO GET ALONG. Some will suggest this is nothing new—and they would be right. From the first moment of rebellion against a loving God, the cracks appeared in our relationships. Ever since, our ugly unlovingness has chipped and jackhammered at the beauty of God's creation.

But it's getting worse.

Or so it seems.

Is it because there are now seven-plus billion of us that the planet seems louder? Or that the Web, "the biggest media revolution since the printing press,"[1] has left us more connected than ever—but also much angrier? Whatever the reasons—and there are many—the cracks in our broken world are showing: Common ground once shared is shrinking. Slight disagreements now carve deep divides. Conversations instantly polarize. We use technology to bully and bash those we've never met. We have grown insensitive *and* hypersensitive. Life teeters always on the edge of outrage. Shocking violence—in word and deed—shocks us less and less. In disgust and defeat, many now refer to these developments as "the new normal."

But is that our only option? To merely shake our heads at what is happening? Surely there are still those who would forge a different path. If things are truly coming apart, the time for action is now. Harvard professor Dean Williams makes this observation in the opening pages of his book:

> What we repeatedly see are systems breaking down—be they institutional systems, economic systems, political systems, or environmental systems, to name but a few—and we all frustratingly ask, "Where is the leadership?"[2]

Where indeed?

It is time for the followers of Jesus to lead. With humility and courage, we must enter the chaos. Loving those who struggle in these uncertain times, we must—and here's the point of the book—love one another, too. For we who sing of grace and preach the gospel will not accomplish much if we do not love one another well. As we will see, this way of loving was the plan all along. To a world splintering into pieces, this different way of relating matters. It is not just a better way; it is the ancient—older than ancient—way of loving another. We who have been called by the Father, rescued by the Son, and empowered by the Spirit are now to reflect the love that flows between the three.

This is how we will lead.

This is how the gospel will still be heard in this loud and angry world. We cannot bring an end to all conflict and patch up every difference. But such love is as winsome and healing as anything we humans can imagine.

To some, such talk sounds terribly naive. "The problems of today are more complicated than some lofty ideal." To others it just sounds too emotional. "Is this going to end in a group hug and s'mores around the campfire?"

No. No group hugs. I promise.

But I am inviting you to let down your guard—just a little. Do you remember a time when you saw Christians reflecting unity? A resilience to their relationships? Even for a season? For most, even a sighting of—dare I say it—*community* leaves us aching for more, wondering if more is possible. But then there are those who behold such things and are forever convinced this is the way to live.

I saw it happen with fifty white folding chairs.

In the early days of The Crossing, where I now pastor, God began to call me out of the marketplace and into my current role. It was a long, unlikely, and unconventional journey that had begun many years earlier. Robin—my wife—and I had become part of this church that started in a living room and was now gathering each week in the community theater of a YMCA. At the time, I was not the pastor of this barely born congregation. No one was the pastor. Not anymore. For various reasons, this little start-up had never really started—at least not in the way we'd hoped. In some ways, it just seemed as though this particular dream wasn't going to take hold. Not in our community. Not this time. What had started with such promise was seriously stalling.

These were good people—big-heart, big-vision people—but there weren't that many left. And now they were without a pastor. By this time, I'd already sensed God tugging me into ministry, in part because of these people. But I figured I'd just end up someplace else. If this church needed anything, it was a fresh face. A reboot.

Or maybe a memorial service.

I was helping to lead these leaderless gatherings, and a few of us had a crazy idea: Why not have everyone come up on that stage and sit in a big circle? People felt sheepish at first, but it was a lot cozier than being swallowed up by a theater that was never going to fill. We sang. We prayed. We opened Scripture. All the things you'd expect in such a time. However, everyone was wondering the same thing: *Are we crazy for caring this much? For praying this hard? Giving this much? Should we keep doing this?*

But then quietly, gently at first, people offered words from deep places. Memories of God's mighty work. Stories of forgiveness. Answered prayer and steadfast friendship. Faith in Jesus inspired by the faith of someone on that stage. Neighbors being noticed and loved. A lucrative career opportunity in another city turned down to remain a part of this family. A whole community entering the grief of a couple whose hearts had been shattered with the death of their newborn, and later celebrating the birth of the couple's second child.

Each time, a powerful story. Each time it was God's work, his doing. But each time, another theme emerged: He had given us the gift of one another for this time and this calling.

It was a gut-check moment. *Could we predict what would happen next?* Not even a little. *Would we pull away from this little dream God had given us?* Not this crew. We laughed. We cried. We prayed some more. And along the way we remembered that God had not just called us to this work. He had called us to this work *together*. We looked at one another in that circle of chairs and vowed to pursue God *together*. We needed him desperately. But now, looking into familiar faces, we were saying that we needed one another.

I said to myself: *With friends like these, I can stand against the darkness.*

And who knows, maybe even pastor them.

Since that awkward, holy meeting, God has blessed our church in many ways. Most of those people have had front-row seats for it all—though never again on white folding chairs. Over the years, some of those sitting on the stage that night have moved away. Some have moved on to other churches. A few have now died. But I am forever grateful that on that day, in that unlikely place, those friends reminded me that we who follow Jesus have been called to an extraordinary work. *Together.*

This is how we will lead.

Or not.

I also remember another time. I was a small boy riding home in the back seat of our car. That's when I heard my mom ask my dad through tears, "How can Christians treat one another that way?"

I'm guessing you know what she means. Perhaps as you read this book, you will fight against an old memory or a fresh wound from a fellow believer. Unfortunately, most of us have those stories.

We have to admit the sad truth: We have forgotten how to get along. Whether we've read through the reams of research that really are piling up[3] or have simply eyeballed the situation, most of us are willing to admit that something is often missing within the Christian community: The way we do life together isn't working. People of all ages are becoming disillusioned with shallow community, disrespectful tones, and the inability to get much done together.

Great. Here we go. Am I just one more voice telling

you that the church is broken and three weeks from next Tuesday the whole thing is going to fall apart, leaving hollowed-out cathedrals and frightened pastors foraging on the forest floor for food? Um, no. I hope not. This is not some hypernegative, "let's all pile on because Christians are the problem" book.

Does "the church" need some fixing? Do we followers of Jesus need to change? Sure. But that shouldn't surprise us. The church has always been in need of repair. As long as broken people keep stumbling into the Kingdom and not-fully-arrived Christians keep following Jesus, this is going to be messy. We will be in constant need of fixing and healing and even reforming. But for God's grace, the church wouldn't have made it out of the first century, much less to three weeks from next Tuesday.

So there will be no piling on. Just a few honest admissions. We Christians are certainly a part of the problem, but we also have a unique opportunity to be a radical part of the answer—an answer that bridges the gaps of generation, denomination, race, economics, culture, and even politics. That seems like too much to hope for, but it's not if Jesus knew what he was talking about.

In this book, we're going to journey together through many experiences converging on one painfully obvious, life-changing, team-building, relationship-healing principle. These various experiences include a lifetime of observing human behavior; a sermon that challenged me to think deeper about the Hebrew word for *one*;[4] the written work of several authors (N. T. Wright regarding the Shema as the foundation for community and John Ortberg regarding pretty much everything);[5] the privilege of leading a fledgling, now-established church with droves of volunteers; the teaching and training of gifted leaders and mentors across the spectrum; and the making of a boatload of mistakes.

It's important for me to say that last part at the outset of this journey. As you read these pages, you will be tempted to say things such as, "I'll bet he doesn't always do it that way" or "There's no way his church practices what he preaches." And you know what? On certain days and in certain circumstances, you'd be absolutely right. I wish I were better at this. I wish the team I'm so grateful to lead were better at this. While writing this book, I wish I hadn't been haunted by the silly and serious mistakes I've made along the way. I am not speaking as one who has mastered this completely. As you've no doubt figured out by now, this isn't my genius we'll be celebrating and considering. It is the sheer and wondrous genius of God.

That's why, even with that confession, I make no apologies for what's to follow. This is how a team, a community, a church works. How it's supposed to work. And on the good days, it does. On one of those not-so-good days when your humanness unleashes its ugliness, this vision of relationship is also how you get back on track. The deeper into this thoroughly biblical idea you go, the more top of mind it becomes, the faster you actually start to make those midcourse or midday or sometimes midconversation corrections. Because this is the better way. The older-than-ancient way of loving.

And it works. And I hope this book, broken into three sections, will help. Here's how.

We first need to tackle "The Mystery"—the mystery and genius of God—before we delve into the practical moments lived out in real time. (For those who are more "nuts and boltsy," your section is coming later.) We will consider one of the mind-bending realities of our faith. But don't despair—this doesn't mean it will be mind-numbing. This could actually be interesting!

(At this point I feel like the middle-school math teacher trying to keep the back row awake: Algebra is cool! If you put enough exclamation points behind a statement, it does sound exciting! Theology can be fun!!! Section one will be fun!!!)

A deeper understanding of God will give us a clearer view of why the way we treat one another matters so much and how our lives fit together. Therefore, section one is definitely worth your attention.

The next section, "Nuts and Bolts," will explore the various aspects of what it will mean to live out the mystery. Each chapter addresses a particular value found in Scripture that is key to us living differently in these fractured times. For example: a healthy culture, humility, the power of words, what it means to collaborate, and entering the chaos and hurt of another. It's not an exhaustive list by any means, but it's a place to begin.

Interspersed throughout are stories: shark diving; a scary moment in a train station in India; sitting in a refugee tent on the Syrian border; staring into a cobra's eyes; even some of the behind-the-scenes moments working in Ferguson, Missouri, before, during, and after the grand jury announcement regarding the shooting of Michael Brown. These stories are all true, and God is still teaching me through each of them. But they are my stories. Hopefully, they will stir your imagination and start conversations around that next step God is calling you to take.

Then, finally, the last section: "The Rest of the Dream." It's only one chapter because there's still much to be written—stories yet to live and tell. But if what has preceded makes any sense at all, this chapter will offer specific ideas for how each of us can take this wild vision of God's even further. It is time for a revolution of sorts. And this will involve some risk. But those God-ordained, faith-fueled steps you take could change the world. I really believe this. I'm not suggesting this *book* will change the world. But I do think it can encourage partnerships between people and organizations, who by the grace of God and of his Spirit working through them could still change the world.

I know that what I've just described sounds overwhelmingly global, but in the end, this journey will be intensely personal. This is how we will lead—by how we love.

Before the great I Am spoke blazing galaxies into existence, there was (and still is) something confronting us. And the sheer beauty of this truth—the genius of it, if you will—won't just change you and me (though it most certainly does that). It actually begins to shape the world around us. You might even say that this is one of the ways in which God is still repairing this fractured world. It is perhaps one of the most tangible ways that others will hear his voice—or at least begin to listen for his voice. It is how we will reflect the glorious transcendence of our God into the dark corners and deep chasms of our day.

Now it is time to scoot to the edge of our own white folding chairs and listen. To think hard and stay honest. To pray big prayers. For the moment is coming soon for us to act—to live and love differently. Our gracious God is summoning us to a different, better, older-than-ancient way, and this way will not be boring because, essentially, none of this is about us. It is about the infinite, all-powerful God who cannot be contained by our three-pound brains. *That's* where the genius comes in. It's him. Always him.

FOR REFLECTION AND DISCUSSION

What divisions do you see in our world today?

What has been your experience with Christian community?

In your own words, why is unity within the church important?

THE
MYSTERY

1

THE WORST NIGHT OF SOMEONE ELSE'S LIFE

The Prayer Prayed for Us

WHAT I KNOW ABOUT LOVING AND LIVING with others has taken too long to find its way into my stubborn, struggling heart. The lessons learned from friendships and ex-friendships, from fellow pastors and those in our church, from leading and following, from forgetting and regretting, from trusting and then watching the timeless God work in real time in the real world—these lessons have little by little taken hold. For this does not happen all at once, this new way, this not-of-this-world way.

And yet, in this frustrating slowness, some truths shoulder their way in suddenly, demanding to be noticed. Not so much in, as one man in my church puts it, "a fork in the brain" moment (which you simply must not try at home) but more in an "ah, of course" moment. Something so right, so perfectly true, that it seems to have been there all along (it probably was), and you wonder how you'd missed it for so long (the reasons are many). But now that it has crashed into the crowded room of your thoughts, it must be faced. It must be dealt with.

For me, this sudden, almost blinding awareness of the obvious happened on the worst night of someone else's life.

THICKENING LAYERS OF SADNESS

There is so much swirling in the room this evening that no one can keep up with his own emotions, much less have the margin to deal with another's. No one except the host. He has welcomed his friends warmly.

That part isn't new. But something is different. By the end of the evening, even the slowest to notice has finally caught up. Thickening layers of sadness weigh on his soul. Something very personal lurks in the shadows of the near future.

Have you ever been near such a thing? Maybe it was a surgery for which the odds were so poor that you couldn't say them out loud. Maybe it was a solitary sentencing before the judge. Or an appointment with the attorney. Or the boss. Or the funeral home. Stand with someone at the edge of a singular storm like that and you'll hear: "Dear God, I don't want to walk through that door . . . but I have to." And he or she does. By God's grace, that person does.

This night is that kind of night.

For Jesus.

The days leading up were a whirlwind of controversy. It is the week of Passover, the great feast of Israel, which always draws huge crowds to Jerusalem. On Sunday, Jesus symbolically declared his Messiahship by riding into the city on a donkey.[1] The impromptu parade had been laced with celebration and danger. The religious leaders opposing Jesus looked on with disgust and fear, but they did nothing. When later he cleared the Temple and called out their corruption, they made up their minds: They began looking for a way to kill him.[2] But how would this happen?

It wasn't long before they had their answer: Judas, one of the Twelve, would deliver Jesus to his enemies away from the crowds and any danger of a riot. As the others would soon learn, on this night, evil would have its moment. But first, one last night for Jesus with his beloved friends.

By the time we get to John 17, so much has already happened that evening. So much has been said. An already important supper, the Passover, was now drenched with new meaning by this one who spoke as if death were waiting outside the door. Of course it was. There was always a cross at the end of this last visit to Jerusalem, but this night it is closer than ever before, this death beyond all deaths.

Then a confrontation with Judas brings awkward closure: blunt words, a gesture, and perhaps one final look from Jesus that broke the heart of heaven, if not the hardened Judas. The betrayer leaves the table for the last time. It has begun.

The unholy kiss, the unjust arrest, the scattering of these overmatched friends, the travesty of his trials, blasphemy in the air, and blood on a cross. It's all coming and soon.

The supper is over. Peter, thinking too highly of himself, receives a haunting prediction of his threefold denial. The glorious truths of John 14 are shared. And then Jesus says, "Come now; let us leave."[3]

A conversation that began around the table appears to have spilled over into another walk with Jesus through the streets of Jerusalem.[4] Something is happening; a darkness is gathering—you can see its shadow on Jesus' face. You can almost feel it creeping its way through the city, trying to find them. After the safety of being together in that upper room, even stepping into the street seems dangerous. They stay close to Jesus.

In those fleeting moments now flying past them all, before all hell is going to break loose, what does Jesus do? When there is nothing else to say to them or at least nothing else their hearts could stand to hear, what does Jesus do?

He prays. Somewhere before crossing the brook of Kidron and making his way up that hill to a grove of olive trees called Gethsemane, he looks toward heaven.

The relationship between God the Father and God the Son is best seen in these moments of prayer. Often, others did not even hear those prayers—they just observed from a distance. Who knows, perhaps this communion between Jesus and his Abba was more than we mortals could handle. But this time, for our sake, we hear the prayer and catch a glimpse of the inner workings of eternity.

FATHER, THE TIME HAS COME

In the sovereign mind of God, this sliver of time to which all of eternity is tethered has finally come. This night Jesus faced, and the darkness that would follow, were not some shocking developments. This was no surprise. Instead, all the details and storylines, all the prophecies and longings, are rushing together, arriving on time, just as God intended.

For quite a while, these disciples had heard Jesus talk about his mission. Why he had come to them. Why he was sent by his Father. But never have the words seemed more urgent. Every breath matters. Every second, one tick closer. All of eternity has been counting down to a moment in time on which everything will turn, and now, on this night, the time has come. So Jesus prays. He prays for himself. He prays for his followers—those with him and those yet to come. And ever present is this grand and glorious mission to rescue humanity and restore creation. It is front and center on this horrible, holy night. But woven into that very big plan is the most intimate of threads holding it all together: the love between this Son and his Father.

"Father..."

So often we talk of this tender term and think of how Jesus taught us to pray. But let's not forget that Jesus and his Abba enjoyed this intimacy before the foundations of the earth were laid. Before we look to how much God loves us, we must begin with the love going on within the Trinity— the love between Father, Son, and Spirit.

Everything flows out of this love. So close are they, so unified in, well, everything.

Though Father and Son are different persons, there is such a sameness to their nature that Jesus had just told the disciples around the supper table, "When you see me, you've seen the Father."[5] The connection between them was so strong, so vital, so safe and wholly pure, that Jesus would pray, "All I have is yours and all you have is mine."[6] Different persons and yet so together that it defies description. We are on the edge of an eternal truth that the writers of Scripture could only begin to imagine.

"Glorify your Son, that your Son may glorify you."[7]

The disciples are overhearing Jesus as he reaches into eternity past, speaking of wonders too great for their mortal minds. This is the way things were "before the world began,"[8] the way things will be again when Jesus returns to his Father's side. But is it too much to think the disciples heard a longing, perhaps an ache, in Jesus' voice? Soon the prayer of Gethsemane will be on his lips. He must face a reality as darkness closes in. Do not forget: This is the worst night of his life. Only this closeness with the Father sustains him. The return to his Father's side calls him. But first, the godforsakenness of the cross awaits.

Jesus was sent here on a mission, and he's now about to take the last painful, glorious step. Looming in the background is what? Love. It was the backdrop for everything that night. It is why Jesus did what he did. It's how he did what he did. His mission was rooted in the intimate goings-on of the Trinity. Would it be too big a surprise to learn that what we do and how we do it should somehow be rooted in the same love going on between Father, Son, and Spirit?

A DIFFERENT PEOPLE

The disciples lean in, for now Jesus is praying for them: "I have revealed you to those whom you gave me out of the world."[9] He prays for their protection from the one who hates everything that God is doing to redeem people and restore his creation. This evil one would use whatever means possible to disrupt and destroy the work and people of God. These precious ones were a gift from the Father. Jesus knows them and loves them. He had protected and guarded them, and they belonged no longer to this world. They belonged to him. They were now set apart as different people with different motives, different ethics, a different mission, a different life. Jesus prays for their continued protection. Why? *So that they may be one* as Jesus and the Father are one.

Soon it would be their mission, and Jesus prays for them to be one.

Soon they would turn Rome on its ear. They were about to do what God called them to do in this world—they would get their hands dirty in this world, loving and serving this world, conversing and sharing with this world *without being mistaken for this world.*

Remember that for a couple of chapters, will you? The people of God are not to be mistaken for this world. Even as the story pushes deeper and deeper into the world. Even as people "from every tribe and tongue and people and nation"[10] become a kaleidoscopic sea of faces that will now form the family of God. This family will now have its share of differing opinions, backgrounds, and perspectives. The people of God will in some ways be just like the world around them.

Only different.

For Jesus now sets his gaze past that dark night to the coming day when this movement would jump the rails and enter the Gentile, non-Jewish world, speeding across the Roman Empire, moving into people groups and languages and cultures and spreading across the ages and continents. With the sovereign plan of a loving God in mind, he keeps praying.

"My prayer is not for them alone. I pray also for those who will believe in me through their message."

EAVESDROPPING

Have you ever heard someone pray for you?

Depending on the setting and the status of your heart, it could be unnerving or humbling or empowering or healing. Sometimes it's all of the above. But when someone starts to speak to God about you, at the very least you ought to listen in. If someone is beseeching the sovereign Lord on the worst night of his or her life and drops your name into that prayer, you'll probably want to listen carefully.

That's exactly what happens at the end of this prayer. Jesus prays for himself and his own mission. Then he prays for his disciples and the trajectory of his movement as it begins to push across the empire. But then he prays for you and me. Of course he doesn't mention us by name, but it's pretty obvious we were on his mind that night—we to whom the testimony of the crucified and risen Savior would one day come. And what is it he wants for us? When his world is crashing in around him, what does Jesus take the time to pray for us?

> My prayer is not for them alone. I pray also
> for those who will believe in me through their
> message, that all of them may be one, Father, just
> as you are in me and I am in you. May they also
> be in us so that the world may believe that you
> have sent me. I have given them the glory that
> you gave me, that they may be one as we are one:
> I in them and you in me. May they be brought
> to complete unity to let the world know that you
> sent me and have loved them even as you have
> loved me.[11]

What is it that matters so much to Jesus in that moment? What is his dream, his longing, his prayer for us? That we will be one as he and his heavenly Father are one. This thread running through the whole prayer now wraps itself around us. He's already prayed this exact thing for those first disciples, but now he asks the Father the same for us.

WHEN SOMETHING MATTERS TO JESUS

With time running out, Jesus didn't pray for his disciples to be brave or persevering. He prayed that they would be one. He didn't pray that we would be clever or compassionate, relevant or intelligent. He didn't pray that we'd win debates or end world hunger. He prayed that we would be one. It must have mattered an awful lot to pray those words on that night. Jesus intentionally lashed this "being one" business to everything he has done and is still doing in this world.

No matter how big and beautiful and colorful and messy the people of God will become, it now comes back to something close and intimate. Jesus prayed for unity. He didn't ask his Father for a bland, homogenized unity but rather for this hodgepodge of redeemed humanity to show the world something outrageously, wonderfully different—so distinctly different that it would cause the world to take notice of God's offer of redemption.

And to do this we must be one.

If that's true, then why do we treat this so casually? Apparently, how we treat one another is directly connected to the very mission of Jesus and the goings-on within the Trinity itself. We can give the world a glimpse into what has always been and what is yet to come.

When we realize that Jesus prayed for this one thing on the worst night of his life, it's going to be awfully hard to not take it seriously.

But to take it seriously, we must first answer a key question: What does it really mean to be one?

FOR REFLECTION AND DISCUSSION

How has prayer helped you in the midst of trial?

What jumps out at you from Jesus' prayer?

What types of behavior keep Jesus followers from living as one?

2

WHEN SHARKS DANCE

The Example Set before Us

SOMETIMES EVEN IN PARADISE you worry things could go
wrong. I was with Robin and our two girls in the Bahamas
a few years ago. I could say we were "suffering for Jesus,"
but that wouldn't be true. At least the suffering part wasn't
true. We were in the land of aquamarine water and beaches
as soft and white as sifted flour. As for the second part, we
were and most assuredly still are "for Jesus" in every way.
Our family is definitely pro-Jesus. And we believe Jesus is
for us. It's why I called out his name through my regulator
in a muffled and bubbly prayer on the ocean floor.

As we've done on other trips together, the four of us
went scuba diving. A friend had referred us to a famous dive
shop that offered to take open-water certified divers off the
coast—to dive with sharks.

Sign me (and my family) up.

There was nothing to worry about—at least that's what they told us while handing us all these release forms to sign our agreement to who knows what in the fine print. With the boat heaving up and down in the Caribbean sun, I didn't have the stomach for reading nor the time to run it past legal, so I just signed the forms.

There would be two dives. For the first one, we dropped into the ocean, descending along a coral shelf peppered with neon-bright fish. This dive gave them a chance to size us up as divers. The guides, I mean. I'm sure the sharks—hovering in the distance at this point—also sized us up, albeit for different reasons.

After this first dive, one of the guides informed us that we would soon see a shark's feeding instinct up close. At this point all three women in my life looked at me with that *What have you gotten us into?* look. You really never want to hear the phrases "shark's feeding instinct" and "up close" in the same sentence. As our dive guide put on a steel mesh suit, a helmet, and steel mesh gloves, I kept wondering, *Where do we get those suits? Was there an upgrade option I missed in that fine print?*

Too late now. Time to go over the checklist. Did my dive buddy (my daughter) and I go over each other's gear? Check. Did I tell my family I loved them and that we'd all laugh about this later? Check. Was it time to start praying really specific prayers? Check.

Then we jumped in the water.

With sharks.

We descended through slow-twisting masses of muscle. The sharks swam in rhythm, waltz-like. Calm but eager.

As if they were waiting for something. They were. We'd been told it'd be best not to do anything sudden on the way down. "Don't draw attention to yourself. Try to blend in, go unnoticed." I never quite understood how to do that while wearing swim fins and an oxygen tank. I tried to look natural, but nothing we were doing was natural.

We were to go to a certain spot on the ocean floor, get into a large circle on our knees, and wait. You could try the one-knee approach if you wanted, but we were told that sometimes a stray shark would see that gap and swim between your legs. (Okay, good to know: Don't try the one-knee approach.) If you fall over, don't reach out. If you panic, don't start swimming to the top. If you need to signal someone, keep your movements very close to your body, if you move at all.

Soon all the instructions made sense.

A steel box opened, and drawn-and-quartered fish came out. The guide (whose extra gear now made sense) speared a chunk of fish flesh and held it at arm's length while he floated in the middle of our circle.

Dinner was served.

The sharks converged on the food, each one thinking only of itself. Many would swim past us, outside the circle, before darting back in. The last thing you wanted was to be a part of this freakish dance. I actually got a head butt from one. He paid no attention to me (another testimony for answered prayer); I was just in the way. I had to readjust my mask, after which I saw the look on the face of Tori, my youngest. *You okay, Dad?* seemed to be the question in her eyes. I carefully gave her a thumbs-up sign very close to my body.

About that time a shark tried sweeping its meal out of the

circle. Alex—my oldest daughter—and I were knocked over. For a very long few seconds, she and I were on the dance floor. We got back up—slowly, just the two of us, with no help from the others. Remember: You're on your own. (Well, *she* wasn't on her own. I guarantee you we did it together.)

I know, I know—you don't win a Father of the Year award for this. But those violent twirls and muscular pirouettes were poetic and terrifying all at once. It was some dance. It was some day in paradise.

A CONFESSION FOR THE AGES

Complete this (loaded) statement:

God is _____ .

There are many great responses, of course. We're talking about the infinite creator of all things here.

Your response says something about what you've learned about God over the years. Or it might reflect what you so desperately need from God these days. If you're new to all of this spiritual talk, you could be working from assumptions based on what you've heard from others. Perhaps the caricatures you've been force-fed from pop culture most affect your answer. Or your response might be a reflection of your upbringing.

A Jewish friend of mine who is earnestly trying to figure out Jesus recently told me, "Here is what I know and believe: God is one." That's where she starts her understanding of God. He is one. That may not roll off the tongue smoothly. It may not even do much for you at first glance (though I'm hoping by the end of this chapter you'll start to think differently), but it is a foundational truth for her. It is what is known as the *Shema*.

Deuteronomy 6:4-9 forms the basis of this confession, this creed of Judaism.[1] For our purposes, we will stay anchored to the glorious and eternal truth found in the opening line of this prayer/confession.

Sh'ma Yisrael, Adonai Eloheinu, Adonai Echad.

Hear O Israel, the Lord our God, the Lord is one.

Beginning with these lines, every devout Jew in the first century would recite the entire confession as dawn broke and again as the sun set. You began and ended your day with this truth. Rabbi Hayim Halevy Donim suggests that the Shema is "the first 'prayer' that [Jewish] children are taught to pray."[2] Is it possible this was the first "prayer" little Jesus was taught?

That's a bit of a brain-twister itself: little Jesus learning to pray. When exactly did Jesus know he was Israel's God come to us? I'll leave that to the scholars.[3] For the sake of our discussion, let's just say that at some point, he knew. He did categorically state he was God come to us, didn't he? "Before Abraham was born, I am."[4] Such extraordinary claims, combined with him walking into the Temple and acting as though he owned the joint (which he did, if you think about it), ended up getting him killed. Along the way, he would explain his actions with these puzzling little stories that, as N. T. Wright suggests, point in the same direction: "Jesus was aware of a call, a vocation, to do and be what, according to the scriptures, only Israel's God gets to do and be."[5] In other words, Jesus really believed this about himself. Only God could accomplish what Jesus would do on the cross.

But first, the humble lowering of himself into humanity. The squeezing of the infinite into the finite. One can hardly take it in—this kind of selfless love. The Word that "shaped the entire cosmos," as John put it,[6] now had to learn how to form words? How much does God love us, anyway? It is almost beyond imagination, but try to see the Son of God crawling into the lap of Joseph or Mary. Imagine what was going on in their minds, these two who knew more than anyone else about that special boy. "This is how we start our day, little one. Worshiping the one true God." Try to imagine the tremors of awe that echoed through the universe when little Jesus spoke what he had known before time began: "Hear, O Israel: The LORD our God is one." Try to imagine the love of the Father hearing these words from human lips formed only a few years earlier—and yet, spoken by an eternal Son who knew no beginning. It's almost too much. God is both above the story and now—like never before—in the story.

Our humble King would grow up saying these words aloud. Not merely because he was a Torah-observant Jew. But because he, above all other human voices, cried out this truth as only he could: "Hear, O Israel: The LORD our God is one." Like no other man or woman who ever spoke these words, Jesus would know what they meant. *God is one.* Do you think it's possible that this was in the back of Jesus' mind while he was praying for us?

Father, may they be one as we are one.

Hear, O Israel: The LORD our God is one.

MORE TO THE ONE

The Lord our God is *echad.* That's the Hebrew word translated as "one." It is a word that has stirred up much conversation in some circles. Since I'm not a Hebrew scholar, I will now tread carefully into non-shark-infested waters (I hope). *Echad* certainly means just what you think it means—"one," as in "not two or three or any other number but one." One and only one. But in some contexts, this particular word also allows for more meaning. In Exodus 24:3, the people answered Moses with one (*echad*) voice—the many who answered collectively as one were a diverse group, but there was unity in their answer. In Ezekiel 37, the prophet who was told by God to do some pretty outrageous things[7] finally got an easy assignment: to take two sticks—one for Judah and one for Israel—and join them together "so they will become one [*echad*] in your hand."[8] This is a picture of a unified one. In Genesis 2:24, we find not only an iconic verse spoken in weddings throughout the ages but also the very first time this word is used in Scripture. What is at the core of God's plan for marriage? That a man would leave his parents so he and his wife can become one flesh. And the word for one? *Echad.*

Sometimes there is more than one in the one.[9]

The use of the word *echad* in the *Shema* is not a proof text for the Trinity. But could these other uses of that word at least invite us to explore the possibility of the mystery of oneness? One more time: *Echad* means "one." *Listen up, Israel, there is one and only one God.* That's the point of the *Shema.* This fledgling nation had just been rescued from Egypt and its many so-called gods. She was about to be led back to Canaan, the land promised to her ancestors. But the Land of Promise was also a land of many gods that would seduce Israel for centuries to come. That's why God warned his people on the way home, "Never forget: I am the one and only God."

This truth does not change throughout the Scriptures.

God is one. What we see, however, as the story progresses, is the fullness of God revealed over time.[10] By the time we get to Paul, Jesus fits perfectly into the oneness of God. Without blinking, Paul writes: "For us there is but one God, the Father, from whom all things came and for whom we live; and there is but one Lord, Jesus Christ, through whom all things came and through whom we live."[11] Paul is dealing with a specific question for a specific church, but theologian Christopher Wright says that in this response, "Paul throws the full weight of the *Shema*—the great Jewish monotheistic confession—at the problem."[12] This thoroughly Jewish Christ follower, writing to a church in Corinth, has just included Jesus in the *Shema*! There is one God. But there is clearly more to him than we can fully grasp or ever imagine. God is one. But (and here we go) he is three-in-the-one.

HARD TO DESCRIBE, EVEN HARDER TO DENY

This is where many Christians unfortunately lose interest. When you talk about the Trinity for more than, oh, let's say a few sentences, people check out. But what if understanding a little more about our triune God is the only way to appreciate what Jesus prayed for us that night? What if that prayer had something to do with those sharks? Would that keep you reading?

Before the sharks, just a bit more theology.

When Christians talk about the Trinity, we're not talking about dividing God up into thirds. Sometimes my Muslim friends think that's what we are saying, but that's not what the New Testament teaches. God is not a pie that can be divided. Nor are we suggesting that Jesus was added as a second God to the Bible—sort of a late-breaking development. This is something against which my Jewish friends so strongly react (and rightfully so, if it were true). But that's not how the New Testament reads. Those early Jewish followers of Jesus never denied that God is one. How could they?

While clinging to the oneness of God, the early Christians also experienced Jesus—who they came to believe *was* God in their midst—praying *to* God, his Father. Then Jesus promised to send the Holy Spirit after he left to be with the Father! This was hard to describe, but no one could deny what they had seen and experienced. Our multidimensional God defies description within our little ol' three-dimensions-plus-time perception. And why wouldn't he defy such limitations? God is beyond the universe he created, so of course he wouldn't fit into any box we could make for him.

And yes, that makes this a mystery of sorts. Does that mean we avoid the tension point between these truths? Not at all. We Christians believe in the God of Israel, who is revealed in Jesus of Nazareth. He spoke and prayed and operated as if he were God come to us. His life, death, and resurrection support that claim. This truth is central to our faith: Jesus is God the Son. But since we are also committed to staying within the guardrails provided by all Scripture, we still proclaim and confess the Lord our God is one. There must be more to the one in the one.

How does that work exactly?

FOR JESUS, THIS IS PERSONAL

Even in the clouded mystery, there are practical handles to grab. God *is* love[13]—sacrificial, collaborative, humble, joyful love in the eternal community we know as our triune God. That's a mouthful, but that's life within the Trinity. We are on the edge of our ability to describe what is happening here, but this is what theologians sometimes call "the dance of the Trinity." What was God doing before, well, anything? Scot McKnight answers with an all-time great quote: "The Father and the Son and the Holy Spirit were in an endless dance of endless love and surging joy and delightful play as they enjoyed the depth of their love for One Another."[14]

This is not just what God does but who God is. The prayer of Jesus in John 17 doesn't mean the Father and Son merely got along and now Jesus just wants us to get along like siblings in the back of a car on our ride into eternity. It is so much more than that. When he prays that we will be one as he and the Father are one, he is referring back to this mystery that *is* God. For Jesus, this is personal. This prayer is about how much he loves and how much he is loved within the Trinity.

And while our hearts should ache with awe at this thought, those same hearts ought to skip a beat when we hear Jesus pray for us. Do you know what this means? Jesus is inviting us into the eternal dance of love between Father, Son, and Spirit. We are not to observe it from the outside, but as redeemed mortals, we are to enter the dance, enveloped in and baptized by God's love, soaked through and through. We will learn again and again what it means to be loved. We will learn again and again (and probably again) what it means to love as God loves, all the while still in this world but not mistaken for it. Encircled by that watching world but distinctly different from it.

Let us not forget that this spectating world was also on Jesus' mind that night: "So that the world may believe that you have sent me."[15] Those who are watching will be intrigued and wooed by a loving God. And according to Jesus, part of this wooing will come by the way we Christians love one another. By the way we dance with one another.

Which brings us back to those sharks.

DIFFERENT WATER, SAME INSTRUCTIONS

Why is swimming with some Christians like swimming with sharks? Why are we so drawn to the first scent of a scandal? Why are we often the first to hit at that juicy chunk of gossip? Why are we so quick to talk behind someone's back, to laugh at the expense of another, to exclude, to demean with such self-righteousness? Why do we think it's okay to treat one another like that? Some would suggest that people who jump into Christian-infested waters be given the same instructions my family heard that day with the sharks: "Watch your back"; "When the fight starts, stay out of the way"; "Don't ever reach out or you'll pull back a stump"; "If you fall down, you're on your own."

When the church fights in ways that would make a shark blush, is it just the way things go—or is something worse happening? It's not just that we are being a little ugly with one another (we are). We are working against what God is doing in this world and treating the prayer of Jesus himself as if it didn't matter. And the watching world? No doubt there are many reasons people ignore the good news of God's grace, but the way we twist and snap at one another doesn't help.

Our credibility isn't the only thing that is torn apart. Who among us hasn't been knocked to the floor or worse? Who hasn't been caught in the middle of something ugly happening between Christians? Who hasn't been hurt? Shocked? Betrayed? When we ignore this prayer of Jesus, it's not just the world circled around us that loses hope. Those of us caught in the feeding frenzy are left damaged and disillusioned by the people of God.

We need to do more than watch this happen time and again. When sharks dance, the twirls and pirouettes are a frightening sight to behold. When Christians dance like this, the heart of God is grieved, his people end up wounded, and a lost world sees more of the same from those who should know better.

There is a better way.

THE DANCE YOU'D LIKE TO JOIN

We are called to be so shockingly, refreshingly different that the world will pay attention. We are to be ministers of reconciliation, not destroyers of *echad*-ness. We are the beloved, and we are to love as we have been loved.

We are to be one.

Some will read this and think such ideas are unrealistic. "Poor Jesus—he just didn't understand how complicated the world would one day be." With all due respect, complicated relationships weren't invented yesterday. God has been dealing with our broken and distorted ways from the beginning. And from the beginning he's been calling us to a different way—friendships that flourish, relationships that last, people who build one another up rather than destroy.

We are to be one.

When this happens, something so winsome, so attractive emerges, it's a relief. It's a joy. It's a ride. And right about then, the world that has circled 'round sees something completely different. A longing is stirred. A hope sparks. And another journey toward the great Jesus begins.

It won't be perfect yet—this community of his followers—and we will talk about that.

But what if we the way we loved actually hinted at something eternal? Wouldn't you be interested in that? Wouldn't the world around you?

Think about it: When sharks dance, who wants to get in the middle of that?

But the dance of the Trinity? Who *wouldn't* want to be in the middle of that?

This is the chance to join something for which our souls have longed—that raucous, healing, life-giving dance. It is the work of God on planet Earth and the work of God in our own relationships. That's why this matters. For the watching world, it is an invitation to consider this Jesus for the first time or the first time in a long time.

But the next loaded question is *how?* How are we to do this?

That's where the sheer genius comes into view.

FOR REFLECTION AND DISCUSSION

Why do Christians treat one another like sharks?

How can you "dance" more like a Christian and less like a shark?

Who are the people in your life—maybe even the difficult people—whom God is calling you to love? What can you do to demonstrate love to them?

3

SHEER GENIUS

The Plan Laid for Us

WHEN YOU'RE HIKING THROUGH THE MOUNTAINS of the American West, it doesn't usually take long for a thick-cushioned quiet to insulate you from the coarse and thumpish noise of the rest of the world. In that new, almost polite stillness, you notice things you wouldn't notice otherwise. Birds competing back and forth for best song. A breeze rasping through the leaves. Honey-colored light dripping through the canopy. That may sound overly romantic, but hikers, hunters, and wide-eyed children know what it is to walk through a wood awestruck.

Pay attention, and creation will always point to the Creator. It declares his glory. Stop long enough, and it gives outright testimony to his genius. Of course, you don't have to be hiking in the mountains to experience this, but it doesn't hurt.

One particular day, our family was hiking with a few other families in a place full of memories for each of us. Working our way up the slope of this mountain, we entered a stand of aspens. That's what you call it—a stand. I don't know why. I understand why we call a grouping of trees "the woods." But why are aspens called a "stand"? Are other trees just a bunch of slackers?

As it turns out, a stand of aspens is a kind of colony of trees, all living off a single root system. All those trees that day—and there were many—were connected to one another. They were functioning as one organism—many distinct trees but still one because they shared the same roots.

That got my attention.

Creation will always point toward the Creator and his genius: "By wisdom the LORD laid the earth's foundations, by understanding he set the heavens in place."[1] Since God knows how things work—how they were designed to work—is it possible we could learn how we are to work together from other aspects of his thoroughly thought-through creation?

ONE AND MANY

The apostle Paul certainly thought so:

> Just as each of us has one body with many members,
> and these members do not all have the same
> function, so in Christ we, though many, form one
> body, and each member belongs to all the others.[2]

It's almost too familiar, this example. But with the metaphor of the human body, Paul offers two realities that will hold us in a godly tension, if we'll allow it: "one" and "many." Both must be acknowledged and celebrated to see the genius of God's plan. Hang on to both, lest you drift to either extreme: a loss of relationships on one end, the loss of self on the other. One extreme leaves you in terrible isolation, the other in utter confusion. Never forget, God knows how things work.

Now let's go back to those aspens.

How many trees were in that stand? Hundreds at least, maybe more. Let's just call it "many." And yet it was just one stand of trees. So which is it? Were the hundreds and hundreds of aspens "many" or were they "one"?

The answer is . . . yes. They were many but still so connected and working together, sharing life together, that they were experiencing a kind of oneness. From what I've been told, an aspen planted alone tends to struggle. Alone, it is more susceptible to disease, drastic weather changes, the stress of living in this world. According to experts, aspens do best in a stand of many trees of various ages and sizes, where the mature provide protection for the young until the young grow past the old. But it is the life that flows between them that is the key.

Is any of this sounding familiar?

The connectedness in a stand of aspens leads to both sturdiness and sensitivity. Carving your initials into the bark of one tree can open the entire colony to disease. But the trees all face that stress together. This is how a stand prevails over time. One colony in western Utah is said to be thousands of years old. At an estimated weight of over six thousand tons, it's also the heaviest known organism. That's how scientists refer to it—as a singular organism. It even has a name: Pando.[3] I for one do not normally name my individual trees or even a most ancient and impressive network of trees. Still, "Pando" has a better ring to it than "stand." This very old root system has seen the rise and fall of civilizations, weathered long stretches of bad weather. And still, after all these years, this particular stand is still standing.

When it comes to aspen trees, their surviving and thriving traces back to their design: the many living as one. Make no mistake: Each is an amazing specimen on its own. The work of an artisan—all those unblinking charcoal eyes sketched on bleached bark. Creation will always point to its creator. But then, stepping back, one begins to see not just the beauty of it all but also the wisdom. Life flowing back and forth between old and young, tall and short, weak and sturdy, established inner-circle trees and pioneers on the fringe. All of this through what is to us an invisible, intricate connection beneath the soil. The many are literally woven together in an unseen but undeniable way.

Sometimes, when we see the many working and thriving as one, we'd better notice the genius of God.

Now back to Paul's point: How many bodies do you have?

This is not a trick question. It's actually pretty straightforward: The answer is one.

How many parts does it have?

This one could be tricky. Just how far down do we break things? Are we talking about basic structural components here? Or an estimate of how many cells are in the human body? How about the various components of those various cells? This could be a difficult number to arrive at. So let me help. Forgive the use of such a technical term, but here goes:

How many parts does your body have? Many. The answer is many.

A GODZILLION IS A LOT

In his book *Your Faithful Brain*, Len Matheson, a neuro-rehabilitation psychologist, cites how multiple sources speak to the impressive nature of the human brain. The young adult brain has about 100 billion neurons, each with between 1,000 and 30,000 connections to other neurons, plus about 900 billion support cells. If we stay conservative—as in the minimum number of connections for all 100 billion neurons—we get to 100 trillion connections. If we open it up to the possible patterns and combinations of patterns, Dr. Matheson suggests we get to numbers we really can't fathom. In fact, not only do scientists not know how many connections are possible in the human brain, but there also are more than they can measure.[4] That's why Dr. Matheson came up with his own word: *Godzillion*. It's the uncountable, beyond-our-wildest-imagination, can't-measure-it number of possible neural connections in the human brain.

The sheer uncountable number of neural connections helps explain how fast the brain works. The numbers for how many operations your brain performs every second keep changing as scientists learn more. But let's go with the latest numbers Dr. Matheson gives us: "38,000 trillion operations per second." How big is that? Tap your finger ten times, as fast as you can. That probably took more than a second, but let's say (after a few more cups of coffee) you can tap ten times per second. Now imagine tapping that same very fast finger at that pace, without stopping; how long would it take you to tap 38,000 trillion times?

I'll give you a hint: It's years. Many years—120,414,734 years, to be exact. Which, if you're still with me, means that 38,000 trillion is a really big number.

The simple point here is your brain can handle that many operations per second in every second of your life. Coordinating your life. Keeping the lungs breathing. The heart pumping. The seemingly invisible and mysterious systems of your body working together in a magnificent symphony of life. Touching. Remembering. Tasting. Laughing. Smelling. Hearing. Seeing. Grieving. Solving. Imagining. All of this is orchestrated by a brain that has a Godzillion different potential connections to make it happen.

That's a lot of parts. To consider how they all work together with such beautifully impossible coordination leaves most of us in awe. Including David, whose poetry describes what his limited scientific understanding could not: "For you created my inmost being; you knit me together in my mother's womb. I praise you because I am fearfully and wonderfully made."[5]

We, who simply cannot ascribe this gift of life to mere randomness, declare with David that we were created. "Woven together" is how the poet puts it in the next verse.[6] In the Hebrew, this is a single word that can mean intricately embroidered.[7] Okay, so maybe that's not exactly working for you: You are God's needlepoint. But think about it. You have been woven together with great care, with intentionality, with skill and artistry and the occasional flair for the dramatic.

A LiVER IN THE CORNER OF THE ROOM

Now that you're a little more impressed with you (you're welcome) or, more accurately, the "you" God has so impressively created, what part of this doesn't apply to Paul's description of the body in Romans 12? When Paul keeps talking about "the body of Christ," what's he saying? Clearly we are to consider the ways in which people work together: sharing the load, exchanging information, supporting one another. In this fragmented, hyperindividualistic world, connection to "the body" must be emphasized again and again. At the risk of once more sounding very technical: The foot bone's connected to the leg bone, the leg bone's connected to the hip bone, the hip bone . . . you get the idea. These parts are just parts until they are attached to one another. Your leg, eyeball, or liver is not nearly as impressive (or useful) sitting over there in the corner of the room. *Nor will it survive on its own.* That was never the plan. That's just not how things work.

Of course, that's the point Paul is making. We need one another. By the grace of God, we have been called to God's side. This is where the new life begins. This is what our souls crave—redemption. Restoration. Relationship with the God of all things. But do not miss the rest of God's invitation, for we have been called to one another's side as well. To put David's poetry to Paul's thought: We the redeemed, the body of Christ, have been fearfully and wonderfully knit together by God.

Is that putting too much into the imagery of Paul? I don't think so. Inspired by the one who first breathed life into existence, Paul seems to think that the human body is a perfect metaphor for how we, God's children, are to function together. The minute we forget that is the minute we miss out on the sheer genius of God's design for his church. How is the body of Christ any less a work of art than our own bodies? Was God any less intentional in designing one or the other? Does he know what he's doing or not?

GOBSMACKED

When I held first one and then another little girl in my arms at the time of their births, my heart ached with unspeakable joy and unshakable awe. I couldn't stop praying (or smiling through tears) either time: thanking God for what was tucked in my arms and praying for her future. Asking him to protect my daughter. Begging him for wisdom and courage in the coming years. *This life before me is worthy of my very best and then some.* I would need God's help at every step to love and encourage, to nourish and protect.

I was, from the very first moment, hopelessly in love and utterly gobsmacked.

And why not? This was no longer a textbooky, theoretical description of life. This was real. It was now personal. I was holding a gift in my arms from the giver of all good gifts, and I could barely remember to breathe. God's love intermingled with mine, coursing through a heart overwhelmed. Before me was a swaddled piece of art. How could I not acknowledge this? How could I not celebrate this? Creation will always point to the Creator. Pause long enough and his handiwork will always give testimony to his genius.

But there's another work of art in our midst. God's handiwork is on display in another of his creations that we too often overlook. Or perhaps we are so familiar with her flaws that we take for granted the love with which she, too, was designed.

Why don't I drop to my knees with grateful tears just thinking about the tender care and intricate planning God put into the forming of *the church*—the body of Christ? Why am I not haunted by the same longing to bless her, to treat her with dignity? To celebrate and encourage what God might do through her? Why do my thoughts not sometimes turn to dreams of *her* future?

This network of lives God has woven around us is no mere accident. It is the obvious handiwork of an artisan. The whole fabric of that community was fearfully and wonderfully made. It is as glorious an expression of God's genius as anything we encounter in the rest of creation. Look around you. (Okay, if there's nobody else in the room or you're reading this at some coffee shop full of strangers, don't *literally* look around you.) But spend some time this week noticing the people God has placed close and connected to you. Discover again how shockingly, beautifully different they are from you. Listen for the unpredictable insights and irreplaceable histories that have been stitched together. In the next few days, ask more questions. Hear more stories.

Allow yourself to be a little awestruck or at the very least amused by all the quirky perspectives and impressive abilities represented in those relationships. The people God placed around you are different. And it is often our frustrating and mysterious differences that lend a sturdiness and flexibility to it all. The many working as one is how we face the storms and stresses of time and still get things done in this world.

We, the body of Christ, may not be as cute as a baby wrapped in a cuddly blanket or as visually stunning as a thousand aspens glimmering like gold on a mountainside, but we are still a sight to behold. Or at least we can be. We have work to do. Some must soon face their need for confession or forgiveness. Those who are disconnected and disenchanted will soon need to reach out and try again. By God's grace, perhaps many can begin to hope again. To celebrate this strange assembly of lives and stories he has put together. But each of us must first drop our defenses just a bit to this idea of being one.

THE LIFEBLOOD OF THIS MYSTERY

There's simply no getting around it: We who follow Jesus are like a beautifully woven tapestry—so many different places, colors, opinions, and voices, giving texture and contrast. Yet for all our many differences, we have one thing in common. It is what Paul calls in Philippians 2:1 "fellowship with the Spirit." We are, each of us, the beloved; the Spirit of God is closer than the next breath we take. In fact, he is so close that one of the ways the writers of the New Testament describe our experience of God's Spirit is that he is now in you—guiding, encouraging, comforting, and empowering you. This is the spiritual life, and it is very personal indeed. But as private as this life with God is, it is also deeply communal. Yes, life-giving love now courses through each of us who believes. But that same love also flows between each of us. This is what heals, protects, strengthens, and ultimately connects us. It is the lifeblood of this mystery we call the body of Christ: the love that is the very Spirit of God flowing between us.

Which makes us more than God's needlepoint. Even

more than a beautiful tapestry. We are more like the root system of an ancient stand of aspens surviving through the ages. Or if you prefer, a vast neural network with a God-zillion different opportunities to work together. Either way, we need one another. Our faith cannot be lived out effectively without the energy and influence of others. We will not grow without the friction and encouragement of others. God set it up this way. Our connection to one another is not just how we survive in this world. It is how we will prevail. It is how we will glorify and honor Jesus.

When the world catches sight of that, Jesus says something happens.

Can you imagine what might happen if we were a little awestruck with this work God has done among us? Would we see one another differently? Treat one another differently? Might we offer just one more drop of grace? One fewer caustic critique? Listen to just one more sentence before interrupting? Stay with a difficult situation just a little longer before giving up? Might we be the last ones to pile on and the first to forgive?

This is our calling. God has laid this out. Jesus has prayed this for us. It is more than a sentimental ideal. It is how his Kingdom will prevail in this post-Christian world of ours. It's how others learn of what we know full well. It is how we are reminded we do not have to do this alone (not that we ever could).

It is long past time for us to thank him for this gift of one another. Allow yourself to get a little gobsmacked. For this plan of the "many being one" is worthy of a little gobsmackedness.

After all, it is the sheer genius of God.

FOR REFLECTION AND DISCUSSION

Why is an aspen stand a good metaphor for Christian community?

When in life have you experienced the benefits of working with others?

What excuses do you make or defenses do you set up to avoid building relationships with those around you?

How have your relationships with other Christ followers strengthened your relationship with Jesus?

4

KEEP ONE EYE ON THE FISH, THE OTHER ON THE BEAR

The Challenge Ahead of Us

CULTURE IS A FUNNY WORD. If you watch a lot of movies with subtitles, you might be thought to have *culture*. Depending on just how *cultured* you are, you might actually defend classical music to that head-banging metalhead at work who you've assumed is a part of the drug *culture* (but has really only been influenced by pop *culture*).

But then your doctor called to say you should skip the museum event celebrating other cultures because your throat culture came back positive for infection. Instead, you're to go to bed early and get some rest. Apparently, you'll just have to settle for eating live cultures in your yogurt the next morning.

So you give the tickets to the metalhead.

No wonder *culture* has been called the second-most

complicated word in the English language after *nature*.[1] It is a funny word with many disparate definitions, so what's one more? *Culture* is also defined as "a way of thinking, behaving, or working that exists in a place or organization."[2] Every church, team, small group, or business has one.

Notice how those various organizations all describe people in some sort of relationship with one another. Andy Crouch tells us that culture begins with the recognition of relationship.[3] Of course, there is an ebb and flow to individual relationships; our connections with one another will intensify and then fade over time. This is life in our ever-changing world. But our relationships also exist in larger seas in which there are strong tidal pulls toward certain behaviors and language. Culture affects everyone in that particular environment. Spend some time in someone else's office, home, or church and you will sense it, even if you can't fully put it into words.

Culture consists of the unspoken rules and practices that do not find their way into an employee handbook. You won't find them in the marketing materials or the church program. (Or is it the bulletin? I never know from church to church. Probably a culture thing.) They are not defined in the bylaws. They are not posted in the locker room or the break room. Few would ever sit down and put these rules to paper. But this is *how* things get done.

Edgar Schein is one of the leading theorists in the field of organizational culture. He was also a professor at MIT. He says the culture of a group is "a pattern of shared basic assumptions that was learned by a group as it solved its problems of external adaptation and internal integration."[4]

Because I never went to MIT, I'll need those cookies on a lower shelf to reach them. Let's break it down into two parts:

1. Any organization is busy trying to thrive in the world while welcoming new additions from the world. *This is WHAT they do.* (That's the second half of his sentence.)
2. A pattern of unwritten rules and assumptions start to form in that organization as it tries to accomplish number 1. *This is HOW they do what they do.* (That's the first half.)

One more time. An organization has a "what" and a "how" that in part define them. Of course, "who" is in that organization also makes it unique, but often these first two have a powerful effect on everyone, no matter "who" they are. For now, let's stick with the "what" and "how."

Integrating and training

ORGANIZATION

Accomplishing things in the world

AN ORGANIZATION'S OUTWARD AND INWARD FOCUS

THE WHAT

Schein suggests that *what* an organization does usually encompasses both an outward and an inward focus. Outwardly, they are accomplishing something: adapting and succeeding in the world. Inwardly, they are integrating: welcoming and training those who join their group along the way.

Is it just me or does this sound familiar? This is the well-known mission Jesus gives his followers in Matthew 28:

> Therefore go and make disciples of all nations,
> baptizing them in the name of the Father and of
> the Son and of the Holy Spirit, and teaching them
> to obey everything I have commanded you.[5]

I don't even think you need a degree from MIT to see that this is what we are called to do. As with any culture, this mission has both an outward and inward focus. Go and announce the good news of the resurrected Christ to a world without hope. Along the way, welcome others into the work of God, making disciples, not converts. Why? Well, if the words of Jesus are to be believed, eternity hangs in the balance. But so too does tomorrow. The daily struggle against injustice and exploitation, fear and brokenness, regret and aloneness is also very real. We have been invited to partner with God in what he is still accomplishing on planet Earth.

We have been called by God to get things done in this world. Let's say that again: We are *supposed to get things done* in this world. As image bearers of our Creator God, we have a baked-in ability and inclination to accomplish things. To do things that will last and matter. This is the "what" of our Christian mission. And that "what" is as big as it gets.

It is so big and so important that it will require our best God-empowered efforts to do what needs to be done. We simply cannot lose sight of this.

THE HOW

But in our efforts to keep our eyes on the prize, we some-times ignore other things happening around us. In our drive to get the "really important things" done, we tolerate bad habits. We overlook and justify ugly practices. We let pat-terns of behavior settle into our daily routines. By definition, this is the culture of our group, team, or church. It is *how* we do what we do. It colors and shapes how we treat one another as we do whatever it is that we do. Multinational corporations, successful sports franchises, and elite military units seem to care about this. Now it's our turn to care more.

Changing the "how" will also require our best God-empowered efforts and an intentional awareness of what is happening around us as we do the work of God. By the grace of God, it might be time for us to form new habits and make way for new patterns of behavior to emerge.

HOW THE "HOW" CHANGES

The culture of any group has an element of mystery to it. But if Schein is correct, we share some basic assumptions—things we probably learned from others about how things are done in our particular setting. If some of those assump-tions are not true, then they should be exposed. A friend recently reminded me of one of the sayings of AA that applies here: "You're only as sick as your secrets." To move toward new behavior, we need to admit and confront some of the unspoken assumptions that often lurk in the back-ground, affecting our culture. There are more, to be sure, but by dragging three of these underlying myths into the light, we can take a step toward change.

Myth #1: As long as we are getting the important things done, how we get it done isn't that important.

This first myth is foundational. It has become the basis for many unhealthy patterns throughout the years, and it's a lie. Yes, from evangelizing the lost to serving the least of these, *what* we do matters. There is no question about this. People are hurting. Wrongs must be righted. Truth must be proclaimed. But in this we can be tempted to avoid spending energy on the feely-meely stuff of relationships in favor of investing in what we consider more weighty matters. As long as things actually get done, we'll have plenty of time to hug it out in heaven. Or so the thinking goes.

In our rush to accomplish something significant for God, we have at times left quite a mess in our wake. How many more stories can we tolerate of broken lives piled high behind some so-called ministry success? Are we actually saying it's worth it? Do we think God could possibly be saying that?

This kind of thinking is not only harmful to those within our unhealthy culture but also terribly confusing to the rest of the world. The followers of Jesus simply cannot separate *how* we do what we do from *what* we do because no one else does, including Jesus. To reach back again to the prayer in John 17, our unity—our healthy culture, if you will—is tied to the world believing that God sent Jesus.

This means *how* we do what we do is as missiological as *what* we do. Anything less than this is not just a troublesome assumption but a lie from hell. It must be exposed, for the temptation to justify our actions in the name of God's great work is the beginning of our bad culture. When attitudes are tinged with such a thought, people end up tolerating more and more and accomplishing less and less. It also leads to our second assumption, which has imprisoned more than a few.

Myth #2: It's not worth focusing on the culture of an organization because it will never change anyway.

It's an awkward but important question to ask: Why spend much energy on culture if there's not much you can do about it? Schein suggests that culture is so deeply embedded, people don't even give a second thought to "how" things are being done.[6] The tug is mysterious, under the surface, and yet powerful and pervasive. We start thinking that talking about culture (much less trying to change it) is useless. We might as well be complaining about the wind. As we'll see more than once, language reveals such thinking: "That's just the way it's always been," "It's not worth making waves," or more directly, "That'll never change around here."

But this is precisely what makes the people of God different. We can change. There is another wind that gusts through our lives, more mysterious and powerful by far. With the Spirit's very personal and patient help, we can change. So too can the health of our systems. It will require some hard-nosed but humble choices by each of us. It will take effort on our part—time and energy, too. But it is worth it because things can change.

A NEW DEFAULT SETTING

According to Paul, it is worth being intentional about such matters: "Make my joy complete by being like-minded, having the same love, being one in spirit and purpose."[7]

This is all the work of God, but apparently we can do some things to cultivate, protect, and even repair how we do what we do.

But let's be honest. To be "like-minded" sounds ridiculous, if not impossible. What does Paul mean here? Well, he is not suggesting we shave our heads and wear matching jumpsuits in cultish conformity. Instead, he is exhorting his readers to make a choice: Be like-minded or, more literally, "think the same thing."[8] Share a common focus. A common approach. Think of it as the default setting of your attitude, often seen in the first reaction to something.

For many, the default setting involves two things: (1) seeing the worst and (2) assuming the worst. When our focus is naturally drawn to the worst in someone, we begin to obsess about all those infuriatingly imperfect details in his or her life. This becomes especially seductive when disappointments and disagreements arise. These do not help.

Neither does our tendency to quickly size up the intent of another with very little information. A situation starts brewing, and often we immediately assume the worst motive possible. Are there times when this is indeed the case? Of course. But when we are going to be in community with one another, a default setting of seeing and assuming the worst will not serve us well.

Paul says to change that. Choose a new normal. Set a new default attitude and first reaction centered on what we have in common with other followers of Jesus.

How on earth does that happen?

There's a clue at the beginning of Paul's extraordinary sentence. We set our minds on that which our loving God has done for us: "*If* you have any encouragement from being united with Christ, if any comfort from his love, if any common sharing in the Spirit, if any tenderness and compassion . . ."[9] Paul is saying *if* all these things are true, but the way it's written in the original language, that seems to be a given. So it's more like, "If this has happened to you (*and I happen to know it has*), if God is at work in you (*and I happen to know he is*) then be like-minded."

We have more than a fighting chance (okay, probably not a great choice of words) to change our ways. Why? Because we share the same reality in Christ. We have the presence of God in our lives. Our hearts are being tenderized by his love. We can sense that he is still up to something.

This is what we have in common—we who live in cities and suburbs, we who attend megachurches or house churches and everything in between, we parachurch or church types, millennial or boomer, mainline or evangelical, Protestant or Catholic or Orthodox. Our identity in Christ means more than music tastes, politics, or sports teams. More than race or gender. More than tax brackets, education, or anything else that matters to us. This is where it starts: the love of God lavished on us who deserve none of it. If we are to mind the same thing, let it be this.

Never do we sacrifice doctrinal truth and the conversations that come with it. But as my friend Pete Scazzero asks, while it is good to be zealous for God's truth and right doctrine, "is it possible that in our zeal, we no longer know how to love those who disagree with us?"[10]

Whether we are talking about Kingdom-wide efforts that wrap around the globe, partnerships that stretch across a city, or the daily goings-on of a particular church or organization, it is time. Time to pay closer attention to *how* we say and do things, because a healthy culture will not happen by accident.

But it *can* happen.

It will require bringing those assumptions and mysterious unwritten rules above the surface for closer examination. Vulnerable and honest questions are then met with humble and honest answers. This intentional act must be doused in the love of God himself. Within this framework will emerge a few brave souls who invite more brave souls, none of whom are angry prophets screaming at the rest of the organization. Screaming rarely works. Instead, what your group needs is what we all need: courageous people willing to be held accountable on these new priorities.

Build on what Jesus has done for you. Work at this genius of doing things as one. It's worth it. The coming chapters will cover some very concrete values and behaviors. As things finally get "nuts and boltsy," they will also get personal. But these changes can happen.

Myth #3: The really bad stuff could never happen to us.

There is a passivity in this assumption that applies to just about every matter of life. If you think the bad stuff could never happen, then you sweat too little, save too little, and generally put off doing the hard work in life. But it will find you, the bad stuff. It always does. Those of us who'd rather not think or talk or do anything about our less-than-ideal relational worlds will find that the hard moments still come our way. If we turn a blind eye to these matters, trouble will still find us. That's why the Bible talks about being alert. Watchful. Living with your eyes wide open.

And that, of course, takes us to fly-fishing.

MULTITASKING

I'm not terribly good at it, but I like to fly-fish. For one, it is apparently a rule of the sport that such fishing take place in the untouched splendor of creation. Fly-fishing in a remote region of Alaska is a great example: the rugged glory of land unfamiliar with footprints, a pair of eagles fighting in midair over a salmon, air so clean and cold that its power washes the lungs.

As they say in the real estate business: location, location, location.

I also like the challenge of a thousand different variables coming into play as your eyes focus on a mysterious patch of water holding so much promise. The slack yellow line in your left hand while your right arm tick-tocks in necessary rhythm, stopping on just the right beat as that line snaps to life, rolling out across the glassy bluegreen.

I love to fly-fish.

For me, fly-fishing requires much concentration to not end up entangled in a spiderweb of my own making. The goal is always that perfect cast and then the perfect drift or set or any number of other things. I usually end up getting at least one variable wrong. But there are moments when they all converge with some sort of poetic flourish. Add to that the chance of landing a big fish and I'm hooked—no pun intended. (Okay, maybe it was intended.)

As I mentioned, accomplishing that particular task in front of you requires a great deal of focus. In fact, it becomes so easy to focus on the "goal" that you can easily forget everything else happening around you. Especially when you're catching fish on a gorgeous bend of river.

That's when I notice the bear.

It's happened more than once—several times, actually. But every time is both awe-producing and awfully unsettling. Perhaps you knew this, but Alaskan brown bears are the same species as grizzlies, which means they are scary big. The only difference is where they live and what they eat. These fellas (and gals) stick close to the streams and rivers for their nourishment. And what nourishment there is: Just about the time the bears are trying to fatten up for the winter (how great would that be if "pack on some weight" was your doctor's advice every winter?), the sockeye salmon show up to spawn and then slow down and eventually die (many at the hand—er, paw—of these mammoth beasts).

Because of the interconnectedness of this ecosystem, the occasional human in those streams is theoretically not on the menu. My job is to stay out of their way and to calmly back out of any water that a bear enters. (I'm okay with that. Did I mention how big they are?)

If they do approach, you are to calmly wave your arms and say—and here I'm not kidding— "Hey, bear." I tell you this as an official graduate of what they call "bear school" at a remote camp in Alaska. I have the pin to prove it. And this is what they instruct you to do. No "Hey, how you doin'?" No "Hey, I was here first." Just "Hey, bear." A casual, mostly nonchalant "I just want to make sure you see me, but please don't eat me" greeting.

Now let's not paint the bear to be the bad guy. Truth be told, I'm a big fan of bears. But bears do mean a level of danger, and you must acknowledge this or you could be devoured. No matter how much concentration it takes to fly-fish, no matter how gratifying it is when things go well, you simply cannot forget to look around and respond to potential danger before it becomes real danger. To assume you can only focus on the goal in front of you without ever paying mind to all that is happening around you is not only foolish but also dangerous.

And that brings us back to culture.

AN ENEMY ON THE PROWL

There are forces at play in this world that do not want this Jesus-shaped, God-reflecting way of relating in this world. For these forces, this genius must not be put on display lest it bring glory to the one true God. Lest it get the attention of a world in desperate need of grace. If the mission of the people of God is as wide-reaching and planet-healing as the New Testament seems to declare, then it would only make sense that the enemy of God would try to thwart it at every turn.

Let us never forget that the enemy of God is also our enemy.

Peter, in one of his letters, speaks of this enemy as prowling around like a wild animal (this time a lion) "looking for someone to devour."[11] The context here concerns those who are suffering, specifically their faith. But the warning applies to all of life. So too does the command that precedes it: "Be alert and of sober mind." Be calm and collected about matters and keep your eyes open, for there is one who seeks to devour.

Looking to devour what? If we can never be separated from the love of God as partakers of his grace (one of the truly great promises of Scripture), then what is it that the devil is looking to devour? Our hope, our effectiveness in this world, our perseverance, our joy . . . all of this is on the menu. *But never forget that he will attack the very relationships we have with one another.* What he wants to do, seeks to do, and may have already done is pull us apart or (even better) turn us against one another. If we overlook odd and destructive behavior because this is easier than facing it head-on, trouble will find us. If we ignore bad habits, bad things will begin to happen. Sometimes the really bad things we never thought could happen will happen.

This was the devil's intent all along.

Peter never says to fear the devil. Just pay attention. Watch what's happening. Take appropriate action. Resist him. Confront evil. Ask the risen Jesus for wisdom and protection and you'll get both. But never sit back and think that you and your family, church, or organization will walk through this world unscathed. You can be and will be attacked. The devil's lurking somewhere at the edge of camp right now, prowling, sniffing, looking for an opening. This is the way of our enemy. We need not fear him. But we'd better notice him, and we'd better be intentional about protecting ourselves—including our culture.

It is a funny, mysterious word. But healthy culture is a gift and a blessing. It is worth our efforts because it matters. It is worth our prayers because God is still at work in us. And it is worth protection because it is under attack. Stay focused on the glorious mission in front of you, but stay very aware of what is happening around you. *What* we do and *how* we do what we do—they both matter. This is the way of Jesus.

Keep one eye on the fish and one eye on the bear.

FOR REFLECTION AND DISCUSSION

When it comes to evangelism, why are both the "what" and the "how" important? What happens when we concentrate on one at the expense of the other?

Which of the three myths resonate with you? How have you seen these myths inflict harm in your life?

What tools does the evil one use to distract you from what God is calling you to do?

How can you stay focused on Christ and create a healthy culture within your community?

THE
NUTS
AND
BOLTS

5

A STORY ABOUT GUNS

In the Presence of Humility

THIS IS A STORY ABOUT GUNS. It's not a story about gun violence. It's not a story about what a Christian is supposed to think about guns—though that would be interesting, wouldn't it? It's not even a story about how at my church someone who is against any gun ownership—including really strong water pistols—can worship next to an NRA member who was sitting in a deer stand earlier that day.

Nope. These guns are more personal. The kind of guns that motivate guys to work out or at least fold their arms a certain way when their picture is being taken. If you're still lost (and why wouldn't you be?), I am speaking of one's arms, specifically the upper arms.

A few years ago, I was at a game at Busch Stadium in St. Louis, where I live. I was the guest of someone whose foundation has done pretty incredible work in serving some extraordinary young men and women in our community. Albert and Deidre would be the first to tell you God has blessed their family in many ways. One of those very personal blessings led to their foundation serving and celebrating children with Down syndrome and their families. On this particular evening, my wife and I were invited to enjoy the game in one of those suites that pastors just don't make it to all that often. We would be joined by some kids and their families who are connected to the work of the foundation. It's usually quite a party, with most folks not paying attention to the game until Albert came to the plate.

But there we were, hanging out with these kids (who also play baseball), and I couldn't help but notice how much they celebrated one another. They also talked very openly about how well they could each hit a baseball, and I got the sense that some of them, like most athletes, might've been laying it on a little thick. But that's what we guys do—we get excited about things like that.

I was playing along—laughing and listening to all their stories. At some point I said, "Well of course you can hit the long ball"—I pointed to his muscular arms—"look at those guns on you." He laughed and gave me a little pose and pretty much agreed with me. I love that. Why not admit something when it's true?

But then he did something I'll never forget. He grabbed my hand and led me to the other side of the room—there was just no other option but to follow. Along the way, he said, "You've got to see this guy's guns." To be honest, his friend's arms really were bigger. At this point he began to celebrate this friend so openly, so boldly: "You should see him play—he can reaaally hit the ball hard." Now it was someone else's turn to agree with the truth. That friend stood there and took it all in. He didn't try to deflect what was being said. He didn't deny it. I watched those words go straight to his heart. Not to be outdone, he eventually pointed to the first young man and said, "But you should see him *throw* the ball. Nobody throws it farther than my friend." Back and forth it went—laughter and stories, friends celebrating one another. It was sheer joy to watch the whole thing play out. Loving words and genuine delight flowing straight from one heart to another. Faces beaming, smiles exploding, heads nodding, arms slung over each other's shoulders.

Something holy was happening in front of me.

If we are to reflect the love that has flowed between Father, Son, and Spirit since before there was time, then surely this was a reflection of that. It was an ordinary moment: two friends having fun, talking about sports. But it was the everydayness of that moment that shocked me. What was happening *was* something that happened every day for them. You could sense it, see it, hear it. This was how they treated each other even when no one else was around. It was, for them, perfectly natural. But for me, it was anything but natural. Not in my world. Unfortunately, not always in my heart. Delighting in the gifts of a friend. Deferring with great joy to another. I was a little in awe of these two. This was how life is supposed to work. My soul ached for what I beheld. But for it to be a part of my life on a regular basis, for it to ever become "natural" to me, would require something truly supernatural.

But it can happen. In fact, it is the key to this different

way of working and living together. And it's found in the two passages from Paul we've been bouncing between in recent chapters.

THE INGREDIENT THAT'S ALWAYS IN THE MIX

The example of the human body in Romans 12 has the many parts functioning as one. This is the genius of God, who has stitched us together with all our various stories, abilities, and viewpoints. This is the work of God, but Philippians 2 seems to suggest there is a choice in all of this. *Be like-minded.* Make the conscious decision to cultivate this kind of unity.

So far, so good. But it is now time for the painfully practical (and personal). In both passages we find the same key ingredient for living out this connectedness. Right before Paul's amazing riff on how a body works come these words: "Do not think of yourself more highly than you ought, but rather think of yourself with sober judgment, in accordance with the measure of faith God has distributed to each of you."[1]

The foundation for the "many" working as "one" is this: Don't think too highly of yourself. If all these parts are going to work together in a symphony of cooperation, then every one of us needs to make sure we don't get a big head.

I wish Paul would just say what he's really thinking.

Hold that uncomfortable thought and jump over to Philippians. What he infers in the first passage he says outright in the second. After Paul has told his readers to be intentional about unity, he writes: "Do nothing out of selfish ambition or vain conceit. Rather, in humility value others above yourselves."[2] Do you see it? The one word to which this all boils down? It's there in both passages. Trinity-reflecting, soul-satisfying, awe-producing relationships will always have this ingredient in the mix. To see firsthand the genius of God, Paul offers a powerful insight:

Start with humility. It's an ingredient in all loving communities.

Several authors and a great many thinkers throughout the centuries have weighed in, some writing entire volumes on humility. Apparently we have much to learn, or we keep forgetting much about this most tricky of character traits.

The reason we find ourselves going back to humility is partly because it is a core attribute of God. The Scriptures are full of examples pointing to this humble and self-giving love. John Ortberg, in his very fine chapter on oneness and life within the Trinity, describes that life as "a community of greater humility, servanthood, mutual submission, and delight."[3] While this does not *seem* natural to us—serving? submitting? delighting?—it is perfectly natural to our super-natural God. This is how relationships were meant to be, how they can be, and how they will be when fully restored by God. It is how he has always existed. Ortberg then points to Neil Plantinga, who writes about life at the center of the universe: "The persons within God exalt each other, commune with each other, defer to one another."[4] There it is again: life within the Trinity. The completely confident and glori-ously powerful persons of Father, Son, and Spirit actively celebrating and yielding to one another.

I think I saw something like that at a baseball game.

Let me say again: This kind of humility is a core attribute of our indescribable God. But its absence is also a telltale sign of our rebellion against him. Pride went before Satan's steep fall and Eden's tragic day. It hangs on every defiant choice we make against God. On most days, the conversations and actions of our world reek with the stench of pride.

It is why humility is so shocking. It clears the air. We can breathe again. We simply don't know what to do with it in its purest form except marvel at it. And perhaps yearn for more.

But now let's do more than yearn.

ONE TELLTALE SIGN

As I mentioned, there are many aspects to what Paul calls "the mindset of Christ Jesus."[5] But for the sake of our conversation, let's just zero in on one consequence of being like-minded with Jesus: *Humility in its purest form will champion the other.* It gives way to an honest celebrating that gives God the glory for the creation of that other person standing in front of you—his or her accomplishments, abilities, very existence. *You praise God and celebrate that person even when he or she has more of something than you do.*

Be aware. For such an extraordinary thing to become a bit more ordinary in our lives will require disciplined action empowered by God. A practical step to take in this area starts with our thoughts. Both the Scripture passages we looked at highlight how we think about ourselves and others. This comes as no surprise because Scripture was making a point about our thoughts long before psychologists spoke of cognitive behavioral therapy. Of course our thought lives matter. Jesus himself stressed this in the Sermon on the Mount when he talked about the seriousness of angry and lustful thoughts. Thoughts have consequences, and frankly, they color our perspectives, shape our reactions, leak into our words, and ignite our behaviors. To get to a place of championing the other, our inner thought lives deserve some attention.

This is not always easy. Some of my thoughts lodged in deep places are downright embarrassing. Shocking. Childish. It's difficult enough to admit to myself, much less anyone else—including God. But this is the intentional groundwork of humility. For God's healing presence to enter prideful thoughts and attitudes, we need to start telling the truth to ourselves about ourselves. Along the way, we will encounter what Scazzero describes as our "shadow." It is, he writes, "the accumulation of untamed emotions, less-than-pure motives and thoughts that, while largely unconscious, strongly influence and shape your behaviors."[6]

It's not easy facing those thoughts, but it is necessary.

A SOBRIETY CHECK

The bloated, self-centered, self-righteous ones will need a strong dose of reality: "Do not think of yourself more highly than you ought, but rather think of yourself with sober judgment." The word translated as *sober* means "to be of sound mind"—you know, sober.[7] What's the opposite of that? Irrational, out of control—you know, drunk. Probably not exactly what Paul was saying, but let's stay with it for a minute. One of the most dangerous things about even slightly drunk people is they often think *more highly* of themselves than they should. They think they're smarter, quicker, better looking, funnier, stronger, you name it. People who overestimate everything about themselves are not just pathetic but also potentially dangerous.

So now the difficult question for each of us: When was the last time you were a bit tipsy with pride? It's never pretty when it happens. When you or I think more highly of ourselves than we ought, predictable and familiar behaviors emerge. But there is one that never shows up: the genuine celebration of another. When you've been sipping from the putrid cocktail of pride, all of life is a competition. Stir in a raging insecurity or two, and enough will never be enough—unless it's just a little bit more than what others have.

Such an approach to this life is a no-win proposition. God always gives his gifts and blessings as he sees fit. And that guarantees that the people in your life will have more of certain things and do other things better than you. This is the truth for all of us. To demand otherwise sets us up for failure: We will never be happy with ourselves, and we can never possibly be happy for one another. Nor will we give God any glory or gratitude for what he's done for any of us. This is why prideful and insecure people (those two really do go hand in hand) have such a hard time experiencing true joy.

Plus, it's exhausting.

There are ways to sober up. It starts with a painful self-assessment, then a resolve. Start telling the truth to God, to yourself, and when it's applicable, to others: "I've got a problem here with my professional jealousy. My self-pity. My fear. The creepy Christiany put-downs that fall out of my mouth. The fact that I hate my friends succeeding." So we pray. "God, I've got a problem, and it's got to stop."

But then take whatever action is necessary around this.

Ask for someone to hold you accountable. You'll be surprised how helpful it is to say these things out loud. Drag it into the light with a trusted friend or a Christian counselor. Ask a pastor to pray for you—and then keep praying about this. Steep your thoughts in Scripture. Read good books by solid authors on this subject (there are many). Cultivate an awareness of how much the all-knowing, all-powerful God loves you. But do something expecting God to meet you there. Remember, this isn't going to happen without his intervention.

What follows is not a step-by-step plan. It is never that easy. But these simple disciplines might get you started.

SIMPLE DISCIPLINES

"I Don't Know"

Learn to say these three words to yourself, to God, and then—when you're really ready to take a radical step toward humility—to someone else:

"I don't know."

Steven Levitt and Stephan Dubner make a painful point in their book *Think Like a Freak*: "It has long been said that the three hardest words to say in the English language are *I love you*. We heartily disagree! For most people, it is much harder to say *I don't know*."[8] They cited researchers who found that the vast majority of children would rather make up answers to unanswerable questions than admit they didn't know.

I'm not sure we ever grow out of that. How often do we stumble through a casual conversation without admitting we really have no idea what people are talking about? Why is it so hard for me to admit I'm completely clueless about that movie or book or current event? If we are not very good in those low-stakes moments, what happens when the stakes are much, much higher? Less-than-humble people almost never say those words. Why? Because prideful people are never without the answer; the political stance; the doctrine; the way you should mow your grass, work out, or carve the turkey. You name it, they will have (and usually share) an opinion about what you are saying, doing, or writing. They are also rarely teachable. How can they be taught? They don't know what they don't know.

Notice I keep saying "they" as though I'm referring to some other saps who aren't in the room. Surely it isn't one of us.

But it is each of us, and it has surely been me.

While there is still much to do in healing my prideful thoughts, I'm trying to implement this one simple discipline: to admit what I don't know more often. It's quite a jolt to the system. A caution here: It's easier to admit your ignorance about things you don't care about. ("I really don't know what the capital of Kerplakistan is.") The moment of truth is when we admit our ignorance about something that does matter. But this is how we learn. This is what it means to be teachable. This is part of being humble.

Ask More Questions

A natural companion to the first is this second seemingly simple step. You will hear this suggested throughout the book, and it sounds so basic that you'll be tempted to skip it. And yes, as with everything that we're discussing, it will be so easy to do this from a place of false humility and posturing. Do a heart check on this one. Don't go through the motions. Do take the first conscious step of cultivating a curiosity. Don't fake an interest in someone.

Whatever the average number of questions you ask in a conversation, increase it by a question or two. You'll actually find yourself become a better listener. Michael P. Nichols, in his book *The Lost Art of Listening*, suggests that "the good listener isn't a passive receptor but an active, open one, attuned and inquiring."[9] It's a beautiful thing to cultivate a genuine curiosity about others. As creatures made in the image of God, the people before you today hold great treasures of story, experience, and wisdom. From them you will learn many things. You will also be inspired and intrigued. It's quite possible that you'll eventually discover something of someone's story that intersects quite nicely with your own. But you'll never know if you don't ask. I have simply lost count of how many times I have walked away amazed at a conversation with someone I barely knew or had assumed I knew. But very rarely did that happen without intentional, genuine questions.

This is not about giving someone the third degree. It's unreasonable and more than a little weird to immediately dive into the deeper waters. "So why don't you tell me about your biggest moments of hurt while we stand here at this party together?" The goal is not to pull things out of someone who is either not ready or willing. Neither is this about manipulating the conversation so someone thinks he or she is being heard, when all you're really doing is waiting for that individual to return the favor and ask you about your much more interesting life. (Isn't it amazing how quickly we can twist a simple act of kindness into something self-focused?) This is about you learning to be genuinely interested in the life of someone else.

It is here that eyes light up and the pace of a conversation gathers speed. The principal goal is not merely to have a great conversation (though there's nothing wrong with that). To ask more genuine questions opens the door to your thought life. Somewhere along the way, you begin to realize that this person has more texture, more depth, more dimension—more story.

When it's your turn (if you get a turn), do not withhold your story. That would be selfish, not selfless. It is your turn to give a little. And when a moment, a comment, comes back your way, don't deflect that glory. Putting yourself down does not raise up the other. When someone delights in you, stop. Just stop. Sense the pleasure of God in you. Then give him the glory he's due. You are fearfully and wonderfully made.

Humility is not self-loathing. Those two young men at the game celebrated each other without such nonsense. They didn't have to hate their own selves to love and elevate each other. Were they old enough to have their own doubts and struggles? I promise you that is so. Had they been exposed to the unkindness of this world? I can only imagine that is true as well. But still, they were both all too willing to bask in their own moment when truth was being spoken about their separate abilities. Is this not what must occur in greater effect within the Trinity—the gloriously perfect and powerful beings who will not deny the truth of who they are, while confidently choosing to serve and celebrate each other? We rarely see this combination of power and deference, of confidence and humility, but this is the standard.

Thus our call is not to water down our own ambitions lest we get big heads. Scripture does not tell us to aim low in this life. The push is against *selfish ambition*. Such an attitude will leave hurt and conflict in its wake every time. But ambition connected to what God is doing in this world is completely different. Such ambition is not panicked or insecure, because we are part of the bigger story happening in God's universe. Instead, it's settled and confident, even relaxed. If it's not all about me, then it's not all up to me.

To be humble means, in part, that I will not forget that God has graciously called me to something—but I cannot forget he has also called you. As we ask one another questions, our stories are told and heard. It is here that we will find at least one thing to celebrate together: the ongoing work of God in our lives and our world. But it is more than a moment of honest delight (though this world is starved enough of real delight). Our stories, told and heard, lay the foundation for Kingdom endeavors. Now we can dream better. We'll spend less energy posturing and instead risk involvement with one another. As we openly and honestly admit our dependence on God, our hearts begin to forge a kind of courage. This leads to that selfless delight in the other.

And that delight leads to worship: "God, I see you doing a little something in my adult child's life. In my friend's life. In the life of someone I don't even know or necessarily like that much. Something good is happening at that other church or in that ministry. I'm going to celebrate that because it's you." You have to choose this way of thinking, but when you do, God meets you there. As always, his Spirit breathes life into that obedience. And somehow, as you take that first step, your heart commingles with the very heart of God. This is what it means to champion and celebrate another. This is the humble love of our triune God.

IN THE SHADOW OF THE CROSS

> Here is a trustworthy saying that deserves full
> acceptance: Christ Jesus came into the world
> to save sinners—of whom I am the worst.
>
> 1 TIMOTHY 1:15

This is the most sobering of statements. Paul writes these words to his protégé not as a new Christian but as a follower of Jesus for many years. It is ever-present before him: Paul is a sinner in desperate need of rescue, and only the sacrifice of God will do. And it happened! God did rescue Paul. He readily tells Timothy in the previous verse that "the grace of our Lord was poured out on me abundantly."[10] For Paul, these two sobering, healing thoughts are never far from his mind: *I am a sinner. Jesus died for me.* This is how he lived—standing in the shadow of the Cross.

So too should we.

How terribly I need God's grace. How wondrously I am loved. I live in the tension between both of those truths. Tim Keller writes, "The Christian gospel is that I am so flawed that Jesus had to die for me, yet I am so loved and valued that Jesus was glad to die for me."[11] It's both. Always both.

To deal with pride on our way to humility requires us to come to the Cross again and again. Standing in its shadow destroys that pride and heals our insecurity. Or as Keller memorably states, "It undermines both swaggering and sniveling."[12]

Now on the heels of this rushes another thought: The very same is true for you. God is just as delighted in you. You, too, are broken. You are also just as prized. And now we are close to the meaning of the phrase some of you choked on a few pages earlier: "consider others better than yourselves."

Some scholars have suggested this means we should defer to others or give them a better place.[13] It doesn't mean we are worthless slugs with no value—no sniveling here. The King of Glory died for us. This is our intrinsic value.

In the shadow of the Cross, a confident humility gives way to glorious possibilities. Among them emerges a deliberate decision to celebrate and, yes, champion other beloved sons or daughters of the King. We will give them a better place at the table:

- Let them bask in the light without elbowing in for a little.
- Tell God what an extraordinary job he's doing with them.
- Pray bold prayers for their success.
- Celebrate when your friend's child does something well—even better than your child.
- Teach your face to smile when someone else knows more than you do.
- Tell people to their face what they do really well.
- Then tell everyone else what they do well.

This is not the way some of us would naturally move, but it's the way of Jesus. We will need much help. This is why we must trust and pray for his help and the Spirit within. When old stuff and familiar voices haunt our thoughts (and they will), we beg God to free us one more time. Then we take another step. All of this takes so much grace. But thank God, he's got plenty. Thank God he offered it to me. And thank God he put you in my life.

These are the words, the thoughts, that should be in our heads and on our lips. This is what will infuse our churches

and teams and friendships with joy. It is the ice-cold anti-
dote to the sting of jealousy. It is the warm embrace that
thaws the odd awkwardness of rivals.

This is what two young champions taught me one night.
No pretense. No agendas. Joy. Love. Humility. It was pure
and shocking—holy. I walked away thinking that this must
be what heaven is like. When I am healed of all the ridiculous things that keep me from being more like Jesus, I'll
know who I am and how deeply I am loved—and that will
be enough. I'll be content and thrilled and grateful and joyful. And I will not hesitate for one second to celebrate all
that is great and good in you. All for the glory of the generous Father who has blessed us both. Why wait till heaven
for this? *God, please create in us what I saw that night.*

And that may be the first story about guns on which we
can all agree.

FOR REFLECTION AND DISCUSSION

How have you personally experienced the negative
consequences of pride?

What keeps you from celebrating the accomplishments
of others?

What habits can you adopt to become a better listener?

Whom has God placed in your life who can help you grow
in humility?

6

AT SOME POINT ALL
OF OUR MOVIES STINK

The Hard Work of Collaboration

THERE IS NO *I* IN TEAMWORK.

How's that for some inspiration? You've no doubt come across this little gem, whether it was in a locker room speech or on a motivational poster. Depending on your current level of cynicism, you just politely grinned, rolled your eyes, or threw up a little in your mouth while reading it one more time.

Whatever your response, I'm guessing that opening line didn't take your breath away.

Why? Because the meaning first poured into those words has long since leaked out. Through use and overuse by well-meaning leaders and lazy communicators, that statement has mostly become a punch line to a joke. But it is still true: There really is no *I* in teamwork. Of course, there's no *U* in teamwork either. (Forgive the grammar and spelling, but who's actually on the team if not *U* or *I*?)

Of course we are on the team. That is the essence of Jesus' prayer for us in John 17. It is the point of Paul's biology lessons in the twelfth chapters of Romans and 1 Corinthians. By God's design, we have been woven together. We are a "team," but a team unlike any other. For our purposes, let's use another word that has its own dangers of being overused these days: *collaboration*.

For several years, teams and organizations have worked to increase collaboration. And why not? It certainly sounds like the right thing to do. Often it is. But what does it actually look like to collaborate, and how does it fit within the framework of our current discussion? If God's plan for his people all along has been for us to work as an organic network of interdependent pieces, then surely we of all people should know what it is to collaborate.

But do we?

Or better yet, do we understand both the extreme benefits and the potential risks of collaboration? Rather than resorting to tired and trendy terms, how can we consciously pursue a specific type of collaboration?

At The Crossing, we have recently sifted through our cultural values with the hopes of making what seems obvious to some more clear to all. This by itself is a part of pursuing and cultivating our culture. One of those values that kept emerging was what we have identified as "creative collaboration." Of course, both of those are fun-sounding buzzwords in the start-up era of Google, Facebook, and Silicon Valley, but what does creative collaboration look like in our worlds?

ECHOES OF GENESIS

Let's start with the obvious: To collaborate literally means "to co-labor, to work together."[1] After all, "two are better than one, because they have a good return for their labor."[2] This is common sense. The writer of Ecclesiastes elegantly reveals even more advantages of collaborating in his fourth chapter. But let's stay with his first statement. Those who work together have a good return for their efforts. The Hebrew word translated as "good" is the same one used in the creation narrative of Genesis as God declared things "good" and eventually "very good." Is it too much to think that as we co-labor together, one of the advantages—one of the returns or rewards—of our collaboration might be something so pleasant and satisfying and rich that it, too, might be declared "good"?

This is creative collaboration, and we were made for it. The fusion of our Spirit-derived gifts leads to something new that would not exist had we not co-labored. Paul is taking us many layers deeper than the Hebrew philosopher we just read. Of course "two are better than one," but in our now-familiar passage in Romans, Paul says "the many" who function as "the one" have become something new. We do not merely share labor; we have become something new and living and creative in its own right. Each of us brings specific abilities, perspectives, and ideas to the mix, coming together to dream, solve, serve, and accomplish. We have different gifts according to the grace given to each of us, as Paul says in the next verses—and we should use them! For when we do, something happens in this world, in the Kingdom of God, that was not there before. And if inspired by and infused with the Spirit, this new thing, this resulting creation from our combined efforts, is good. Anything with our fingerprints on it will not be perfect, but such a thing can be so good it gives honor to the one true Creator.

Let's try it this way: If God is still up to something in this world (and he surely is), there will be moments of creative genius born out of his people. But these moments will not always or even usually be spontaneous phenomena. They will require effort. They will require pursuit. They will require cultivation in order to bloom. It is one thing to dream big. It is quite another to watch those dreams take form in reality. This is the "good reward" of creative collaboration.

YOU NEED A BRAINTRUST

But do we followers of Jesus invite one another to share new and challenging thoughts? Will we take the risk of divulging ideas so impossible that only God could make it so? When a heartfelt idea is on the table, will we risk sharing helpful feedback? Can we hear such feedback when it's our idea? To think of ourselves with sober judgment is not just the humble acknowledgment of our own limitations; it is the open-eyed awareness of how badly we need the other "members of the body." In other words, your talents and ideas just won't be as good without those other talents and ideas.

I told you we'd start with the obvious.

Now what does this actually look like? In his book *Creativity, Inc.*, Ed Catmull describes a type of creative collaboration that was birthed by the Pixar movie classic *Toy Story*.[3] I'm not sure which of the adventures of Woody, Buzz, and company was your favorite. I have loved each one for different reasons, though I'm ready to admit publicly that I was a mess after *Toy Story 3* and Andy's departure for college. Seriously, who cries over talking toys in a children's movie? Me, that's who. Such is the power of a story well told. (Well, that and having to drop one of my own girls off at college.)

What most didn't realize until Catmull's book was that something called "the Braintrust" has become an essential element of Pixar's continued success. This collaboration started with the five men who oversaw the production of the original *Toy Story*. In the ensuing years, the Braintrust has morphed into a larger group of creative storytellers who meet every few months to review current projects, identify problems, and offer potential solutions. Pixar now relies on this process to "push us toward excellence and to root out mediocrity."[4]

That last sentence sounded intense. For some who are convinced the church has slid over the edge of the entertainment cliff, *excellence* is still a good word for us. Is this not the natural by-product of worship? If a life with Jesus in charge is a life brimming to the very lip of human capacity, how do we not offer our best at every turn? How can we not expect that our best Jesus-led, Spirit-filled moments will yield anything but excellence? It seems only logical that we would also want to "root out mediocrity"! Doesn't the Kingdom deserve such efforts?

Of course it does, but our fears and biases linger. While we're at it, do not let the word *creative* trip you up, lest you assume this is another diatribe about the need for slick programming and singers who sing on pitch. I assure you it is not. (Though I do think worship leaders who sing on pitch are generally a good idea). Remember: What we do matters. But how we do what we do matters. And the "what" and the "how" are inextricably connected. This is as true for a community-wide literacy program as it is for anything happening on a Sunday morning. It's time for us to collaborate with the full intent of creating something extraordinary together for the glory of God.

Some might object, "I don't consider myself a creative person. I don't write poetry or make pottery. I don't play an instrument. I don't paint or sketch or doodle. I don't even own a beret." Ah, but if you are now a child of the King, then you have been imbued with his presence—and when you bring his gifts to mix with what he has given to others, you can create. Technically, it will always be him doing the creating, but you get to be part of something more beautiful than anything you could ever accomplish on your own.

And that takes us back to Pixar's Braintrust.

THE VULNERABLE MOMENT OF TRUTH

Apparently, one of the key ingredients in these collaborations is what Catmull calls "candor."[5] For the Braintrust, candor is the freedom and responsibility to share the truth with one another about upcoming movies. This often unfiltered (but hopefully not unkind) feedback allows for better-informed decisions and—I might add—better-formed ideas. Having to explain and even defend an idea to a trusted and supportive audience makes me think better. Such candor also forges the path from mediocrity to excellence because there is now a collective creativity in play. If

I might apply the words of Paul here, candor allows the many working as one to create.

But for this co-laboring to be most effective, the truth must flow both ways.

I must share the unvarnished truth of my idea before you can fully speak your truth about it to me. If I want my dream made better, I must first share it with you in all its incomplete glory. It is important to articulate and even defend that idea outside my own head, where just about everything of mine sounds brilliant. This is the bracing moment when that hopeful thought is brought out of the gray matter and into the light. It is the intimidating moment when I lay my best attempt at something before others, knowing that it is less than finished, less than excellent, and still tinged with much mediocrity. It is the heartbeat-skipping instant when a longing is revealed and a dream is confessed. It is yet one more act of humility where I admit I won't see this fully realized without you. But before your truth can help me, I must show you the truth about me and my ideas. I would prefer that you agree with me at this juncture, but in my best moments I begin to realize you will make my contribution better with one of your own.

IT COULD GO EITHER WAY

This is a powerfully vulnerable step. But only then will candor have its full effect. Much now hangs in the balance. This most difficult decision to share my dream can happen in the blink of an eye. But in the blink after that blink, many things can happen. Fear is no longer a giant lurking in the shadows. It is now fully visible and fully felt. Just check your pulse when you speak up and share that big idea with others. A risk was taken, and fear is present. But now, in the light, that idea can be felled with the right word from others. If the first words are at least kind and respectful, then what happens next will not destroy. Truth is still coming, but it will not cut to the core even as it stings.

If you're the person hearing the idea, the easiest thing to do is offer an opinion. But opinions are cheap. It's why the world is full of them. The genius comes when you bring yourself into the dream with me. When others begin to lovingly offer not just observations but also their own ideas that weave into mine, we are now co-laboring—and two (or more) definitely feels better than one.

Notice this, for we are now standing on the edge of a kind of creation, something new in this universe. So much good is so close to being unleashed. But these flickers of creation happen fast and can be quickly lost. A mocking tone, a dismissive word—and everyone retreats to safer places. Silently everyone vows to remember what just happened. This is now marked as unsafe territory for new ideas and unfinished dreams. Better to protect the status quo than risk being singled out.

Teams that tolerate this behavior will eventually complain that things are stale and stuck. Soon they will blame one another or their audience, their clients, their congregation, or their world. There will be no fresh solutions to the aching problems of the day. There will be no teamwork because there is barely a team. There will be no harmony now. No surprising turn in the middle of the song that breathes new life into an old desire. Instead, there will be the same tired, blaring solos that everyone knows by heart.

SAY IT OUT LOUD

There is risk in collaboration. And that risk must be acknowledged even as it is managed. There's a term used by many (I first heard it from Nancy Beach), perhaps first coined by Roger von Oech,[6] that speaks of both risk and protection. It is called "the umbrella of mercy." At our church, our team speaks this phrase aloud before someone shares an unfinished or particularly vulnerable idea in any number of meetings or conversations. As in, "I'll need the umbrella for this one . . ." This means two things: (1) I am now taking a risk in sharing an idea with you, and (2) you will honor that risk with your next words. In addition to asking for the umbrella, I've been known to request "galoshes of mercy." (Such is the state of my psyche at times.)

There's nothing magical about the umbrella of grace. Invoking it can easily devolve into mere ritual, a silly incantation of meaninglessness. But for our team, these words still mean something. We want to both admit the risk and respect the acknowledgment of it. But why is such vulnerability even worth it? What is the return on all this extra effort to maintain such safety? Again, Catmull captures the thought succinctly: "Early on, *all* of our movies [stink]."[7] (Except he uses a coarser word than *stink*.) These creators of one memorable movie after another openly admit that early on, their efforts aren't so impressive. This blunt assessment has humility and even a touch of desperation to it.

Does that sound familiar? This is certainly true of my endeavors and probably yours as well. In its initial stages, my idea just might, well, stink. Not at the core, hopefully, but at the very least it's not what it could be and will be when others are invited to contribute. This bold expression of humility and desperation must now be voiced inside faith communities. Often.

The challenges we face are both exciting and daunting. We must now be humble and maybe desperate enough to ask one another for help. This is not a pep talk about teamwork; it's a warning integral to our survival in this post-Christian world. It is necessary for you and me to collaborate because none of us has cornered the market on all gifts and abilities. This should be painfully obvious to all but the most prideful among us. (Please do not tell me you have "all the spiritual gifts.") There is much to address in our God-starved world, but we can't do this without others. Of course. You know that. But remember, this is not just about sharing a workload. It is about creating something together that wouldn't exist without our collaboration. You will make my contribution better with one of your own. But there's another equally pressing truth about our need for one another, and it, too, will show up rather quickly.

We each have blind spots. When it comes to my ideas, I can easily get lost. I'll need someone's help to see a more complete picture, because I have blind spots. We all do— parts of us we just can't see. Like our teeth. At a party. Where they're serving dip with chives. Or anything that lodges itself in that tiniest of nooks between two front teeth. You'll never know it's there, but everyone else will. No one will notice your clever party banter. No one will notice your casual but cool fashion choices. You're just someone with something in your teeth.

My wife and I have a strategy for such situations. (I'm sure it's not original. If we heard it from you, we both thank you.) If we see some piece of produce flapping from the other's teeth, we simply ask, "How's your mother?" A sweet, innocuous question asked in public that for us sets off a clanging silent alarm: "Get thee to a mirror quickly. Floss, brush, extricate, expectorate, do what needs to be done, but until then smile with pursed lips." If I sense that I'm in danger of displaying recent food choices, I can also ask Robin, "How's my mother?" At that point she will tell me (a) my mother's fine or (b) I should probably check on her . . . now.

I don't like it all that much when Robin lovingly tells me I've got something in my teeth. It's frustrating and initially embarrassing. I like to fancy myself as the dashing and intriguing life of the party. But compared to the longer view of going the whole evening in such a state, *I'll always choose the former awkwardness to that latter regret.*

When it comes to our activities within the Kingdom of God, let us never forget that we have blind spots. But let's do our best to take the longer view when receiving loving feedback. Let's seek it out. In the midst of great excitement and even clear vision from God, keep asking a few trusted others the right questions: "What am I missing?" "Where is this not making sense to you?" "How could this be even better?" "Where am I getting lost?" "Am I making this too complicated?"

"How's my mother?"

For it is usually better to choose awkwardness early over regret later.

That doesn't make it easy—just worth it.

IRRITATING ONE ANOTHER TO EXCELLENCE

When the writer of Hebrews tells us to consider how we may spur one another on toward love and good deeds, he's making the same point.[8] The word *spur* means "to rouse to activity or encourage,"[9] but in some contexts it can also mean "to provoke."[10] Which means feedback can irritate quite easily—if that's all it is. But the writer of Hebrews quickly stresses the importance of "not giving up meeting together, as some are in the habit of doing, but encouraging one another—and all the more as you see the Day approaching."[11] We must keep gathering together. Why? To encourage one another face-to-face. Doing so against the backdrop of eternity adds meaning beyond words. There's an urgency to what we do. It matters. But again, how we do what we do matters. So keep encouraging one another as you spur (and slightly irritate) one another toward excellence (and away from mediocrity).

Catmull says that the reason this type of collaboration works at Pixar is that they have "a vested interest in one another's success."[12] The same can be true for the rest of us. Deferring to one another sometimes leads to an undeserved but undeniable payoff. By joining forces in Kingdom endeavors, we are all folded into the great story of God for which we were made. The true genius of our Kingdom collaboration emerges when *your* interests ultimately become *my* interests because they are now *our* interests. It is the only way we can tolerate being spurred on some days.

This makes sense, but the process itself requires a watchful and confident eye. It's essential to curate the various ideas and variations on ideas. Some will find life, and others will fade. But along the way, the group must allow personalities and giftedness to expand and retract. It's often a balancing act between the stronger and the softer voices, the quick and the slow processors, the wonderfully spontaneous and the carefully thoughtful. This is where leadership is needed.

On the edge of creation many variables hang in delicate balance. And so here are a few thoughts on how to spur one another on effectively.

Stir the Pot

We do not control all the elements of creation. How could we? We are but marred images of the true Creator. But in the mystery of a creative moment lies a great responsibility. For new and truly collaborative ideas to bubble to the surface, those with influence and authority must protect and empower those new to the discussion. The most creative stews usually have at least one person who is noticing those on the edges and those in the red-hot center, constantly stirring both into the mix. Such leaders will invite and exhort everyone present to set aside their place on the org chart, the size of their ministry, or their years of experience for the sake of what might happen in the coming moments—*your interests are my interests because they have become our interests.* Often the leader must first model humility for the more powerful while sharing influence with the less than powerful. This is how the pot is stirred.

Mind Your Language

Another way to keep blending the ingredients is to stay mindful of the language used in your setting. This is not about avoiding words that would offend Grandma's tender sensibilities (though that's not necessarily a bad standard). This is an appropriate awareness of tribal language—code words, catchphrases that reach back into the community archives. This is more than good manners; it is good leadership, for speaking in a way that everyone in the room understands is your best chance for true creativity. Otherwise, everyone in the room gets the joke—except the people who don't. Who are they? Usually they are the newest to the conversation, church, or team. They will also have the freshest sets of eyeballs and perhaps the most energy to devote to this project, if invited to do so. Take the time to fold them into the mix. Explain the joke or where the collective groan came from. This will always take longer, but it is your best chance of ushering someone with shockingly fresh ideas into the warm center of the group. It is also one of the humblest things you can do—slow down and explain yourself without frustration. Without condescension. With a self-effacing humor, even.

What about the New Kid?

But what about when you are the new kid on the block or in the room? On the one hand, it can be intimidating, and some of what has already been said about risk applies. This team needs you, and you were more than likely brought to them for such a moment as this. But depending on your outlook, you might actually enter this new partnership with a prideful tone. (Beware the cocktail of pride and insecurity.) It's the old geezers who will soon have trouble keeping up with you. You're the one with the latest technology, the exciting innovations, the best ideas for getting unstuck. You're not that interested in the old joke, the previous failures, and the smarting wounds from recent battles. Now that you're here, it's a new day!

Some of this might be true, but humility is still the foundational ingredient to creative collaboration. This takes us back to the simple act of asking questions. Listen for stories. Learn from those past failures, or you just might repeat them. Do not too easily miss the emotion in someone's eyes when he or she shares that story. Let people show you their scars (figuratively, of course). Some of these lessons being shared did not come cheaply, and you would be wise to slow yourself down. You may have the freshest eyes and a brain full of ideas, but some wisdom only comes from the dents and dings of experience. There will be time to contribute, but first learn. Listen. Remember, you may not be the first person to think about this issue. The goal isn't so much for everyone to take your idea and run with it. It is to work together, which offers the potential for something none of you expected. Start there. When it's time to speak, you'll actually be heard and not just tolerated. And what then results might be something good—even very good.

TWO HUNDRED CUPS OF COFFEE

My friend Jake works for Youth for Christ, and one day I asked him if and when they were going to move into St. Louis to work in some of the urban spaces where we are serving. His answer was quick and memorable. His organization wouldn't even consider such a move until after engaging in much prayer (of course), finding the right opportunity (makes sense), and taking the time to buy two hundred cups of coffee (huh?). Jake said they usually need about two hundred conversations with local leaders, pastors, and people on the ground actually doing Kingdom work in a city before they even know if it's the right step to take. Two hundred time-consuming, one-on-one chances to hear someone's story over a cup of coffee. "We're just the new guys in town. We might have some ideas, but first you tell us what you know. What you see. What you've learned. Then we'll see what we can do together."

Do you have any idea how that sounds to a pastor's ears?

This is what it means to be ruthlessly committed to collaboration. It is not moving in too fast or too hard. It will always have the otherworldly ring of humility to it. It is both vulnerable and safe. Honest and respectful. It is spending precious energy to cultivate a space where the risky moments of sharing a dream can be met by the generous offer to make that dream better, bigger, and more attainable. It will take longer than you want, cost more than you've got, and require more to maintain than you first imagined.

But it's worth it.

There are those who will resist and dismiss this as trendy. While I understand the resistance to gimmicks, look deeper. This is the ancient way. My talents and ideas just won't be as good without other talents and ideas. Two are better than one. Many working together as one is the best. This co-laboring is not always easy. Just better.

If Pixar can figure this out, so too can the people of God. With one teeny-tiny disclaimer.

FOR REFLECTION AND DISCUSSION

What comes to mind when you hear the words "creative collaboration"?

How well do you respond to constructive criticism?

What steps can you take to become more aware of your blind spots?

Whom is God calling you to invite into the creative process?

THE DISCLAIMER

The Hard Work You Do Alone

MUCH HAS BEEN WRITTEN THESE DAYS about artificial intelligence. The dangers and potentials of this emerging technology hover on the near horizon. It's certainly above my level of understanding (and probably my pay grade) to address such matters. But here's what I *can* say about the near future: If the autocorrect function on my phone is any indication, it will still be a few years before robots rule the earth.

You see, my autocorrect is usually more of an overcorrect. A simple text message that contains one innocently misspelled word suddenly becomes shockingly less than innocent. How could the artificial "intelligence" at work within my phone assume this is what I was trying to say? Have I ever said that in a text message? Now my thumbs scurry to carefully type what I meant to say the first time. And how what I did say the first time is not something I would ever say to anyone, anytime. Especially to you, Mom.

What just happened?

While it's fun to joke about a technology's first slumbering steps, let's not kid ourselves. We humans do this all the time. We live in a veritable age of overcorrecting, and we do it almost automatically. Like a new driver in a skid, we wrench the wheel first one way and then the other, always moving (and fast) but mostly fishtailing between extremes. From diet trends to politics to management styles, we are drawn to drastic solutions. Armed with more information than patience, we don't just fix a problem as soon as we identify it. Instead, we keep fixing it until it's a different problem.

How often have you seen someone who, after reading an article or attending a conference, is now ready to foist some sweeping, system-wide solution upon his or her organization? Armed with good intentions and insights, this person is eager to *correct* something, and quickly. How often do these abrupt shifts in focus swing a team in the opposite but equally unwanted direction? And so the fishtailing begins. For some churches and teams, these wide swings happen too often. Do not succumb this time. There is hopefully much truth in what we've already discussed, but heavy-handed turns of the wheel can easily become overcorrections—almost automatically.

Hence the disclaimer.

Over the last few decades, strategic emphasis has gone from silos to mixing vats. From organizational to organic. From cubicle farms to free-range office spaces. From departments that saw one another at the Christmas party to daily meetings in the ball pit at McDonald's. In the pursuit of Silicon Valley ingenuity, people now brainstorm, spitball, and cross-pollinate in one big multidisciplinary play zone.

Is that a good thing?

Some of it could be. But is there a danger of overcorrecting? According to data collected and reported in the *Harvard Business Review*, the time spent by employees in what the researchers call "collaborative activities" has increased by more than 50 percent in the last two decades.[1] According to these researchers, people at many companies now spend about 80 percent of their time participating in meetings or answering colleagues' questions.[2] The opening line of their article sums things up: "Collaboration is taking over the workplace."[3]

Apparently someone got the memo, but again: Is that a good thing?

In our efforts to tear down the barriers and isolation of the past, let's now call out the risk (and even temptation) of overcorrecting. In my own experience with highly collaborative teams or those moving toward more collaboration, there is a very real chance that an overemphasis on us working as one can lead to an underemphasis on each one of us working.

Allow me to explain. There are at least three dangerous assumptions in collaborative environments that can slow a team down. The origins of each may have started with a benign or even well-meaning thought. But still there is potential danger here. If the following assumptions are left unchecked or unquestioned, patterns of behavior grow and intertwine around the ankles and arms of any ministry. What has the potential of breathing life into a team or church can, when overemphasized and misunder-stood, choke and trip that same group with a new set of difficulties. That is why all three assumptions must be continually challenged even as newer ways of interacting are explored.

ASSUMPTION #1: WE MUST DO EVERYTHING TOGETHER

Growing up, my youngest daughter, Tori, played soccer most of her days. It was fun watching her and her team develop over the years. But have you ever watched really young children learn the game? Spacing is nonexistent, positions indistinguishable. Everyone drifts back to the ball like bees to the hive. En masse they move, bumbling and buzzing around the ball, but never really getting anywhere. It's more swarm-ball than soccer.

People on highly collaborative teams love checking in with one another before moving forward. If this is not pos-sible in person, at the very least everyone must weigh in digitally. Since we do things together, we must all see every-thing and then hit Reply All so that we're all in this together. This is what makes us a team.

But is it? Must we do *everything* together?

The danger of *co-laboring* so much of the time is that we forget about the *laboring* part. To go back to our example from the previous chapter, the so-called Braintrust at Pixar does indeed gather to pool their insights and talents to cre-ate something much better than any of them could accom-plish on his own. But those meetings—essential as they are to both the organizational and individual success—happen every few months.[4] Not weeks, not days, but *months*.

Of course, there's no formula for how often people should gather to collaborate effectively. For some, there will be brief or not-so-brief connections daily, depending on the tasks at hand. This connecting with others has a rhythm that is intuited at times and almost mandated at others. But the point of Pixar's approach should not be lost on the rest of us. In between those meetings, something else happens. People do their jobs. They hit deadlines. They make progress—on their own. With that in mind, perhaps it's time to tweak our cliché:

There isn't an *I* in teamwork, but there is *work*.

As in your work. My work. We have individual jobs and roles to which we have been assigned, for which we volunteered, and in many ways to which we have been called. The only way this "working together as one" works is if each one of us works even when we're not together.

Swarm-ball is cute when you're five. But now we need to spread out.

In our particular organization, which *loves* to have many voices in the mix, we've had to assess when it is time to streamline the process. This takes many forms: Take a few people off that particular e-mail stream, reduce the frequency of a standing meeting, and—the really difficult one—uninvite yourself from that project. This will cause a certain amount of angst and uncertainty for some on the team who are used to others thinking for them. It might also bring a sense of loss for the one who's used to being at every party. But this development is a good thing; it begins to challenge the second assumption.

ASSUMPTION #2: CERTAIN PEOPLE MUST BE INVOLVED FOR THE BEST IDEAS OR WORK TO EMERGE

There's often a natural logjam that builds up around certain individuals in any organization or team. Without ever intending to do so, they have now become a hindrance to workflow because of their helpfulness and undeniable usefulness. As the *Harvard Business Review* observes, "Soon helpful employees become institutional bottlenecks."[5] In other words, there are a few people in most organizations with whom everyone loves to work—and for good reason. They work hard. They are fun. They are insightful. Nuggets of brilliance fall out of their heads as soon as they're apprised of a situation. Such teammates don't just succeed—they help *you* succeed.

Who wouldn't want them at a meeting or on a project?

Based on that description, it seems almost foolish to move forward without such input. And sometimes it is foolish—so don't. But the limitations of even the highly talented inevitably emerge. As it turns out, they are human. Their lack of omnipresence makes their constant availability a bit of a struggle. Projects and people needing answers start piling up outside the door of these valuable teammates, leaving them overwhelmed at their inability to help everyone and keep up with their own jobs.

Does this sound familiar to some of you? Being invited into such an intoxicating array of conversations is fun . . . until it isn't. You will run out of gas and ideas. It's only a matter of time. The best part of your day was just spent solving everyone else's problems. Meanwhile your own problems are still waiting patiently for you. No wonder the research is not too optimistic about those who collaborate too much: "They are so overtaxed that they're no longer personally effective."[6]

That can't be what God had in mind.

Meanwhile, those who have grown too dependent on this overcentralized person start panicking at missed deadlines, and ideas aren't as fresh as they used to be. Workflow congeals and frustration seeps to the surface.

It almost seemed easier back in the silos.

However, there is a way to unclog things: *The super collaborator must learn to say no earlier.*

If people are lining up outside your door right now (do you even have a door?), what is keeping you from using that two-letter word? Henry Cloud's very important *Necessary Endings* is worth more than a passing glance. He rightly suggests that "endings often are absolute necessities for a turnaround or for growth to occur."[7] This is not a suggestion that your super-collaborating should come to an end, but that it should become more refined and intentional. Do not allow all this activity to swirl around your schedule and significant abilities.

If at this point you're thinking this particular chapter is a direct contradiction to the last, it is not. It is, however, an essential counterbalance. The nature of effective collaboration is both yes and no. But healthy boundary-setting does not mean saying no to everything. It certainly does not justify a Grumpy McBitterpants routine where you keep telling everyone to get off your respective lawn—at home, work, school, or church. This does not warrant your complete isolation from everyone else so you can "finally get some work done." That would be an overcorrection of a different, crabbier sort.

The rhythmic back and forth of "accept" and "decline" is learned and relearned by the best teams and its members.

This is the genius of working as one to the glory of God. It is both the joy of contributing and the necessary humility in letting others have their shot. *But it is both.*

Cloud reminds us that when the super-collaborator steps back, other opportunities for growth will now have their day. And this leads to the third and final assumption that has lingered far too long in the shadows of every church, team, and organization.

ASSUMPTION #3: IF EVERYONE ELSE DOES HIS OR HER PART, MY PART WON'T MATTER

When the rest of an organization leans too heavily on a particular player, it brings problems to both team and player. In the language of our larger discussion, a body part that is overused runs the risk of injury or at least fatigue. It also means the rest of the body is not functioning as it should. Other parts are underutilized and underdeveloped. This is not an efficient way for the many parts to work as one body. The many end up relying too much on one, and before you know it, you're walking with a limp.

That's why the last section was for those talented people who might just do too much. But now that they are going to back down and steward their collaborating a tad more wisely, it is about to be someone else's turn to contribute.

That could be you.

In this last assumption, the attention now turns away from the super-collaborator and toward the under-contributor. This is the person tempted to assume that the team does not need him or her. Again, in those environments where teamwork is stressed and fostered, there's usually much activity. But in the midst of that buzz, people can hide or get lost. For the overlooked and underappreciated, consider this your official invitation to join the others on the field. It won't be smooth, this transition, and it will require patience as others forget to explain the inside jokes and shortcuts that have existed for years. But don't let that stop you. Even if it appears from the outside that things are moving along swimmingly, you are more needed than you now realize. When certain others on the team actually start establishing more healthy boundaries for themselves, you'll be downright essential.

But there are others in these environments who do less because, well, that's what they always do—less. If that's you (and it's been most of us at some juncture of our lives), hopefully this will serve as an honest but encouraging challenge to reject the lie that is this last assumption.

In 1 Corinthians 12 we see Paul making the same point we've already encountered in his letter to the Romans. God has designed and sovereignly assigned certain gifts and abilities to those who are now a part of what Paul calls collectively "the body of Christ." The mysterious and beautiful harnessing of all these lives is to be celebrated as a whole. But the value of each individual person and every Spirit-breathed gift is also stressed by Paul's favorite metaphor. Here, he has a little fun with the point by having body parts talk to one another: "The eye cannot say to the hand, 'I don't need you!' [Is this what they mean by "bad hand-eye coordination"?] And the head cannot say to the feet, 'I don't need you!'"[8]

Such prideful isolation is not God's design for the body of Christ.

Interdependence is very clearly Paul's main point with this talking anatomy lesson. But implicit in it is the need for every part to actually do what it is supposed to do—whether it be a prominent and highly visible part or not. Paul says the whole body can't be an eye or ear, sure. For all sorts of reasons that would be rather odd and ineffective. No, each part has a job to do, and for the brilliance of God's design to be experienced and enjoyed, *each part must now contribute*. The big toe should understand its value, for the rest of the body needs a big toe (or two). So do your job, big toe. Otherwise things are going to get off-balance quickly. The same goes for those unseen and unsightly internal organs without which we won't make it very long.

To assume we won't be missed is to assume we know better than God how all these parts work together. But we didn't design this body any more than we designed our own. He did. And we don't get to tell him how little our contribution would be missed. After all, "God has placed the parts in the body, every one of them, just as he wanted them to be."[9]

So trust God and do your part.

The beauty of the many working in unison will happen only if we all show up.

Go a little crazy when it comes to creative solutions. Dream big. Have fun. Jump in the ball pit every now and then. Tear down some silos. Make a habit of collaborating.

But beware the overcorrection, because we're not playing swarm-ball. The buzz of activity is not enough. It's time to do your part. Not more than your part. Just your part.

This is how highly collaborative teams get things done. It's how they run fast. It's encouraging. It's often fun. Even when it's not, it's worth it. And because we begin to bring our best to the table, not only do we call great things out of one another, but we also begin to relax a bit. I don't have to do it all. I'm not supposed to do it all. And trust? Well, it starts showing up as never before.

Speaking of trust, let's talk about building it.

FOR REFLECTION AND DISCUSSION

What would it look like to increase your level of productivity?

List habits that will help you become a better worker.

8

LIFE AND DEATH

Grace and Grumbling in Our Words

NOT MUCH GOOD HAPPENS when the foot, eye, and liver are at odds. It's best when we work together. Paul makes this common-sense case brilliantly. The echo of Jesus' prayer is even more compelling: It's best if we work *well* together.

If only that were easy.

You've probably noticed this, but we humans aren't always the cheeriest bunch. The reasons for the unrest will often trace back to legitimate concerns. At other times, the source of our frustration is a rather unflattering truth about us. Most times, however, what's wrong in the world gets tangled with what's wrong in us, leaving us tied up in knots.

However we get there, it happens.

Yes, even we who are redeemed and headed for an eternity with Jesus aren't always happy. (What?!!) It's true. We are dissatisfied about things that happen within churches or between churches or with people in those churches, denominations, or other organizations. This is nothing new. Even in the early, heady, miracle-filled days of the Jesus movement, not everyone was happy in the church.

THE WARTINESS OF US ALL

In Acts 6 you'll find a church that was growing numerically in the face of persecution and enjoying the work of the Spirit in their midst. These early Christians had front-row seats to the power of God. But still, imperfections and unmet expectations remained. Conflict began to swirl around the way people were cared for—widows from a particular demographic, specifically. Whether this was simply a careless oversight in a fast-growing church or the result of an underlying bias, people were being neglected. Either way, this was not good. At-risk women were being ignored right under the apostles' noses. Of all the amazingly positive things the church could celebrate, this was not one of them. And with that, after the first few lumbering, miraculous steps of the Jesus movement, came a legitimate stumble.

It turns out we Christians have a long history of not getting some things right. That is not a cynical observation but a truth to face and expect. There's so very much the followers of Jesus *did* get right—and still do. Sociologist Rodney Stark has done much to clarify the long-standing history of Christians "getting some things right" in this world. Read one of his many helpful books wherein he makes the point convincingly.[1] We Christians have a long and storied legacy of making a difference in this world. There is much good being done by local congregations and multinational relief organizations and everything in between. But until we have been fully restored in the life that is to come, we humans—even we Jesus-following humans—will keep making mistakes. Some innocent. Some tinged with our own residual darkness.

This is where it gets interesting.

In the community of faith, we should admit this rather obvious but painful truth to one another. Not to glory in our fallenness. And not as a preemptive excuse for tomorrow's failures. But rather in preparation for how we will treat one another tomorrow—when one of us fails the other.

When new attenders become more involved in the church I pastor, they will quickly hear stories of our great God at work and the future into which he still calls The Crossing. That is the easy and inspiring part of welcoming people into our community. But we also try to prepare them for the rest of what is to come. Eventually, we will disappoint them at some level. I will disappoint them. To expect otherwise is to foolishly fast-forward to a reality not yet here. We all are firmly anchored in the "already but not yet" of this life until Jesus returns. And that means the closer any of us gets to a particular organization, church, family, or individual, the more visible the warts are on each of us.

Redeemed? Absolutely. Perfect? Not even close.

How we now handle one another's wartiness can make the difference between protecting the *unity* and splintering it. It's often the difference between a trust built and one destroyed. It's the difference between a resilient partnership and a fragile alliance. In many ways, it's the difference between life and death.

There is much that breathes life and death into our relationships with one another. We will now focus on just one nuts-and-bolts aspect. It will be enough to keep us busy for a chapter or two, and then the rest of our lives.

Words.

They matter.

A lot.

THE WEAPON OF CHOICE

Just one or two words can do real damage. String the right ones together in a full sentence and lasting harm results. Proverbs 18:21 tells us the words formed in our mouths have "the power of life and death." Those of us who didn't write Proverbs will say just the opposite, often in an effort to deaden our regret: "I didn't really mean it." "Don't take everything so personally." "Sometimes I just say what I think." "They're just words."

These are feeble attempts to deny what, deep down, we already know: Words have great power. I do not mean here something akin to the incantations of folk magic. The one true God of the universe is not beholden to the utterings of any mere mortal. My words don't cast any kind of "spell" on you, nor do they handcuff the sovereign Lord to any action. But my words can have great effect—on you, me, and us.

Words have, in fact, become the Christian's weapon of choice against other Christians. This sounds absurd—since when do Christ followers intentionally inflict harm on another? Ah, but therein lies the serpent's snare. We all agree violence against another is abhorrent to God. But our words are *just words*. It's the sticks and stones (and more highly developed weapons) that inflict real damage. Words are just words. They can never hurt me or you or us.

Do we really believe that? If so, we're ignoring the clear warnings of God himself. Scripture is filled with vivid and disturbing imagery that describes the potential havoc our words can wreak. It's as if God keeps saying, "If that image doesn't get your attention, does this one bother you?" We find many of these warnings, though not all, in the book of Proverbs.

DISTURBING IMAGES

Proverbs 12:18 warns us that "rash words are like sword thrusts."[2] In the Hebrew, the imagery is quite violent. It is the act of stabbing. Not an inconvenient paper cut but the piercing of flesh. A rash word or two can slice into the heart of another and leave more than a mark. It can leave a gaping wound. This is what sword thrusts do. They leave awful, painful marks. In the aftermath, someone is left bleeding all over the floor.

Too graphic?

Proverbs 15:28 tells us "the mouth of the wicked gushes evil." In the original language this gushing business can refer to something that has fermented. When something ferments, a chemical reaction produces effervescent bubbles. Sometimes those pent-up bubbles explode outward. Something happening on the inside is eventually spewed out. This is the imagery of that word. In the Psalms, it is rendered in some translations as "belched out."[3]

Evil is belched out. Now there's a picture.

If you've ever been around someone who belches loudly

and often, it's disgusting. It's rude. It stinks. And your best instincts tell you to get as far away as possible. There are many forms of evil that spew out of the human mouth. And some specifically damage the unity between us. You and I should pay heed when someone starts belching evil into the room, saying things they shouldn't say, and spraying that ugliness all over anyone nearby. Stay close enough, and those words will land on you, cling to you. Stay long enough in that cloud of yuck and you will soon stink yourself. So will your thoughts and, who knows, eventually even your words. Before long, you'll start belching a little too. This is what happens when evil is sprayed and spewed into a room. It touches everyone.

For the record, when I've said things I shouldn't say, playing dumb does me no good: "Golly! Where did that come from?" I will tell you where it came from. It came from inside me. Or you. Or whoever just belched. It came from someplace deep, where it's been fermenting. After a particularly nasty rant, we Christians try to act shocked by what just "spontaneously" erupted from us, but that is an intellectually dishonest ploy. I actually have a pretty good idea where it came from *if* I'm honest with myself and the God who already knows what's brewing deep inside of me.

I told you this imagery was disturbing.

How about one more?

Right after Paul exhorts us to follow the humble example of our Servant-King in Philippians 2, he reminds us we will not do any of this on our own. It is God who is at work in those who believe and trust in Jesus. As individual believers, we are to live out our faith in everyday moments, always in awe of what God has done for us.

Then, rather bluntly, Paul tells us to get our corporate act together. We will also express our obedience to God in the context of our relationships. And so we read in verse 14, "Do everything without complaining or arguing."[4]

Well, that's asking a bit much, don't you think?

Let's be clear: When the Bible talks about us living at peace with one another, for instance, it is not saying we can never have different ideas or opinions about certain things. Scripture gives us these passages precisely because we will be unhappy when encountering these differences. Nothing in the Bible suggests we will all end up bestest buddies. The key to lasting community is what we do with the wartiness of one another. Again, this is not a call for monolithic conformity where no individual voices are heard. In the first story from Acts 6, Luke tells us the people complained—and for good reason. We aren't told for how long or in what manner, but they complained and their voices were finally heard. Good for them. Good for the church.

I believe what Paul is getting at here is a danger lurking in our words of complaint—for they are habit forming. In some translations you will read that first word rendered as *grumbling*. That's more like it. There is a sort of grumbling that may start off as an observation or legitimate concern, but before long it takes on a life of its own and leads to quite a mess.

Which brings us to the last image. The Greek word here comes from a word that describes the cooing of doves or pigeons. "But I like the sound of doves cooing," you say. But have you ever witnessed up close what is left behind when doves or pigeons are done sitting around? You see what's left after all the cooing and murmuring?

We don't coo much. For us, it is a low murmur, a cynical observation mumbled again and again. It is the caustic comment the rest of the group can't quite hear completely, but they feel the rumble. It is an unsettling grumble that sounds nothing like peaceful cooing. But the resulting mess looks everything like that park bench.

Have you ever been part of a group where this kind of behavior is the norm? Where such messes are left regularly? It's surprising how quickly we grow accustomed to it all. Some will be shocked if you suggest it happens much. People now think nothing of it. It is part of that culture.

Much of the same applies to an argumentative spirit. It's certainly no coincidence that Paul mentions these two in the same breath. They go hand in hand. Someone who makes a habit of grumbling will often argue for the sake of arguing. It, too, is a habit. The chronic arguer will tell you that this is constructive criticism for everyone's benefit, but that person's critiques and retorts are mostly for his or her own amusement and a few select others.

Here lies one of the seductive hooks of this habit. It is never long before someone listens willingly, and the rush of wicked pleasure is palpable. *Someone is affirming my scathing insights? Wait, the room laughs at my acidic putdowns?* When you or I realize there are people willing to play along, the habit begins to form. The back-and-forth grumbling is now like a drug craved and hard to quit.

The mess we habitually leave isn't just in the room we left but in our own hearts. I am really distorting my own feelings about the person or organization that upset me. My nonstop complaining starts to build a case for why I will pull away, why I will never forgive, why I must retaliate. All of these feelings start solidifying the more I share my grumbly words with others. Think about it: We are now increasingly "on record," and the last thing we want is to be wrong on this matter. The more we complain, the more we dig into a place from which we won't soon budge. Such is the power of words.

And we have all done it.

But they're just words. It could be worse . . . It could be worse? How about *we can do better?*

The other sins—the ones that make the headlines—will break the heart of an organization, tear apart a family, or leave a team in ruins. We must guard against these. But so too must we pay attention to the sins of our mouths. Words that cut deeply, comments that fill the room with a foul stench, murmurs that leave behind an undeniable mess—they matter. For this is how most communities die—one toxic sentence at a time.

NEW HABITS

Then what are we to do? Much of this will come down to what festers inside each of us. Such work cannot be avoided. (There was a wise man who once talked about the futility of merely cleaning the outside of a cup.[5]) But as we face these truths, we can take community-wide steps together. Rules of engagement, as it were. What follows is an admittedly incomplete list of practical steps to get you started. There are others, to be sure. Discover them together, and humbly put them in place.

As you start noticing and incorporating new habits into your communal life, notice how they fall under one principle that stretches across the entire New Testament. It guides our thoughts and directs our steps, and now it helps us measure our words.

The Grace-Restored Must Now Be the Grace-Ready

If we enjoy the grace of our loving God, we must offer it to others. Get ready, for the time has come to share it freely. This is the only way our words can heal in the midst of our disappointments.

Wise Words Are Always Connected to Intentional Listening

We turn again to the wisdom of Jesus' little brother, James: "Everyone should be quick to listen, slow to speak and slow to become angry."[6] This is the dance of "one quick and two slows," as John Ortberg puts it.[7] It is a dance that has proven itself over and over in my own life. It is a dance I am still learning. But for starters, learn to listen well. The first step will help you find a rhythm with the other two. Trip here, and you'll never learn the dance. Dietrich Boenhoeffer says it, as always, quite memorably:

> Many people are looking for an ear that will listen.
> They do not find it among Christians, because
> these Christians are talking where they should be
> listening. But he who can no longer listen to his
> brother will soon be no longer listening to God. . . .
> In the end there is nothing left but spiritual chatter.[8]

The discipline of listening is more than not talking. When I listen, I intentionally open myself up to a different perspective. I learn things I didn't know. At the very least, I am now reminded that this one before me is also an image bearer of God. At this point, the knotted ball of irritation in my chest starts unraveling.

Much has been said of the dangers of "objectification."

It is an oft-used word of which you may be tired. Or you may have no idea what it means. Simply put, when someone begins to perceive another person as only an object, that person will treat the other differently—less like a person, more like an object. A woman seen as a sexual object is not treated with honor, but rather as a commodity. A child perceived as a mistake will not be cared for tenderly but will be treated as an inconvenience. Entire people groups have been viewed as dehumanized objects, robbed of all dignity. You can easily see how such thinking leads to the cruelest of behavior.

My words can become a part of this downward cycle toward what Martin Buber called the "I-It" relationship.[9] "That guy? He's the jerk who . . ." "That church? It's a bunch of phonies who deserve . . ." The labels (and loaded ones at that) serve to dehumanize. From here, it's easier to treat someone with less dignity than he or she is due. This person (or persons) has become an "it."

At this point we have forgotten that God is so completely enthralled with this person that he knows the exact number of hairs on his or her head. We are very far indeed from seeing this person as one for whom the King of Glory died. *She's a pain in my side. He's a squeaky wheel that needs silencing. They're a problem that needs fixing.*

But if we listen, we have a very real chance of moving toward what Buber calls the "I-Thou" relationship. Listening reminds me of his or her story. I hear again that individual's name, and if I'll allow myself, I remember how he or she is beloved by God. Listening helps inform my prayers for that person, if I dare. This is not, however, a "Dear God, please clue this idiot into the error of his or her ways" prayer (a dead giveaway for an "I-It" relationship).

Instead, it is usually a halting, less-than-eloquent prayer for someone I probably don't understand all that well. Not yet. But the listening helps. If I pray for this other person *after* I have heard his or her perspective, *my heart has a chance of softening—even if my stance doesn't.* This is an important distinction. My heart can open up even if we still don't agree. How? God meets me there, before any resolution or agreement. This person who is frustrating or disappointing me is becoming more of a person to me. An impressive, imperfect, but prized-in-the-eyes-of-God person. It's "I and Thou," not "I and It."

And with that, my words begin to change.

Take a Breath before You Tweet, Post, Comment, or Hit Send

The rules have changed overnight in our world. Anyone has access to platforms that were unimaginable a generation ago. It used to be that you would have to sit down and write a letter to the editor of your local newspaper and hope that it was conveyed intelligently and with enough decorum for it to be printed for others in your community to read—knowing you wrote it.

If you weren't much of a writer, you could always show up at city hall or voice your opinion to the PTA or a church business meeting. Still, you were there in person. In London, there's still a quaint tradition where you can stand on your soapbox (literally if you'd like) in a corner of Hyde Park and let your words fly. But still, it's the real you. Even the guy off his hinges at the corner bar is a real person who, for better or worse, is attached to his words.

But the rules have changed. We all now have access to a platform larger than any of those mentioned, and with it comes little responsibility. For it is mostly faceless (or at least face-to-face-less). It has the potential to be cowardly and anonymous. The ease of putting those words into the digital universe, coupled with a lack of accountability, has given way to a dangerous uptick of evil belching in our world. From "walls" to "feeds" to the infamous comments sections in some Internet spaces, we have been given a very large soapbox indeed. Among communities in the blogosphere and genuine camaraderie expressed by "friends" and "followers," there are other words in the air. These words are foolish at best and hellish at worst. Those struggling for meaning and standing in the world now have their threats and theories heard. But there's no person behind such words, only a username. And it is too easy to spout and spew our many opinions when we are known to the world only as chucknorrisiscool_598.

Let's not contribute to the stench. Even when there's a form of accountability and our names are fully known, we find it all too easy to type ugly and damaging words. We blow off ugly steam about a person or group and tell one another, "It's only words." Ah, but that's the point. Words matter. A lot. Even the ones we launch from our computers and phones. This includes the searing e-mail.

Take a breath. Let your words sit for a second (or more). Edit them. You might end up deleting the whole thing. Or maybe it is something worth saying and sending. But if that is so, I promise it is worth saying and sending with great care.

I firmly believe that if James were alive today, the "dance" would have another step: quick to listen, slow to speak, slow to anger, *and slower than you are now* to tweet, post, comment, or hit Send.

In the Matter of Life and Death, Pick Life

Right after Proverbs 12:18 tells us that rash words stab like a sword, it tells us that the words of the wise bring healing. This should be our goal. When a legitimate bump in any relationship occurs, our words (backed by action) will make the difference. In our story from Acts 6, the church at large could've easily ignored this small minority, but they didn't. This young growing church listened and responded quickly. In essence they said, *We can't do it all, so something has to change. It wouldn't be right to neglect our calling, but it also isn't right to neglect these widows. You pick the right people. We'll turn it over to them.*

And with those confident but humble words, things began to heal.

Our words—backed with action—have the power to heal. What began to die starts coming to life. The Bible is clear on our general approach to conflict, though there is no cookbook recipe for success, as is sometimes suggested. Our relationships are too complicated for that, and God is too loving and honest to tell us otherwise. But there is redemptive wisdom for these difficult stretches of road. The Proverbs hold such wealth. Paul's teachings are essential. The painfully practical James should be within reach. And ever always, the words of Jesus.

As you might expect, John Ortberg has brilliantly summed up this wisdom in one of his books.[10] If you are looking for a longer and profoundly challenging look at this process, Ken Sande's *The Peacemaker* has helped me in ways I cannot fully put into words. It may also be that a gifted Christian counselor is in order. Or a trained Christian mediator. All of these are now available to the body of Christ. Such resources have been placed in our midst by our loving God, who has knit us together. Remember, many parts working together in this one body—that's the plan. To fully reap the benefits of such godly counsel will require a humble heart. That, too, is the plan.

But above all, love must be our motive.

THE BOOKENDS MATTER

We who are familiar with grace must spend it freely. Eagerly. In a stretch of road I did not want to travel, God put strong loving voices in my life to remind me of this. Always in need of God's grace, I must also offer it. One of those voices was (and still is) a woman of unimposing stature who does not attend our church. If you met her on the street, you'd be struck by her sweet smile and gentle spirit. But do not be fooled by appearances. She will storm hell's gates. An excellent mediator and counselor, she exhibits strength that does not come only from years of experience. It comes from a breathtaking confidence in our God and the Scripture he has given us for such times. It was she who pointed out the context of the oft-mentioned Matthew 18 passage regarding Christians in conflict.

She told me the bookends matter.

On the front end is the parable of a loving shepherd who goes out looking for one lost sheep (you remember that one, don't you?). On the back end is the parable of the unforgiving servant (you might not remember this one, but the point is fairly obvious in response to Peter's question about how many times we are to forgive another). So on one end is the loving pursuit of someone who has strayed. On the other end is the command to forgive because we have been so outrageously forgiven. In the middle is the famous passage about what to do when a brother or sister sins against you.

The bookends matter.

Clearly, I am to forgive as I have been forgiven. The grace-restored must be the grace-ready. There is no other way for us to live with one another's imperfections.

But perhaps I should also follow the lead of my Savior on the front end of this passage. Do I lovingly pursue relationship—even when it is difficult? I must admit this is not always in my sweet spot, but I find God willing to patiently teach me along the way. We do not give up; rather, we pursue. We speak truth directly and privately. We forgive lavishly because we have been forgiven as such. With this, there is a chance.

That is the point of all these words, isn't it? Jesus says in the famous passage on conflict resolution, "If they [your brother or sister] listen to you, you have won them over."[11] This is our goal: a healed relationship. Few things are more difficult to imagine, much less to witness. Few things shout more to the glory of God and the power of his love. These are resurrections happening before you—a relationship once dead now alive.

I have seen this with my own eyes. I still long for it through my own tears. But I still believe it with my own heart. "If it is possible, as far as it depends on you, live at peace with everyone."[12] These moments when our imperfections bump into one another will not be solely up to you. But as much as it is up to you, be at peace with everyone.

Do you know what makes that possible? It is the power

that raised Jesus from the dead. This same power—the Spirit himself—rushes through each of us and connects us to one another. But do you know what is up to you and me?

Our words. Of course there is much more to this. But our words leave doors and windows open for God's healing to move in. Or they close off any real chance at reconciliation. They have that kind of power—the power of life and death.

FOR REFLECTION AND DISCUSSION

What steps can you take to control your speech?

How is God calling you to use your words to build up others?

Choose one of the practical rules from this chapter. How would incorporating this action into your life improve your relationships?

9

THE COLOR OF
A COBRA'S EYES

The Poison of Gossip

I LIKE TO THINK I'm up for an adventure every now and then. I will occasionally land in a situation that Alex, my oldest daughter, calls "iiiinterrresting" (as a reminder, we were the two knocked down by the sharks). I'll leave my issues for a therapist to find someday, but one afternoon in the mysterious land known as India, I might've gone too far.

The day was so hot, the air so saturated, that it seemed to weep on our shirts and skins. I felt as though I were being smothered. To our hosts it just felt like Tuesday.

But in the watery heat of that "normal" day in India, my day was soon anything but normal. As a surprise, our friends had arranged a chance to meet three snake charmers. Off the beaten path in a city most Westerners will never see, our small group now gathered to watch this strange, surreal performance. I am not recommending that you seek this out. Frankly, whether such spectacles should be allowed has become a source of debate and controversy in India. I am not condoning the practice, obviously. But on that little path we encountered something straight out of the movies.

Three men sat cross-legged on the ground. A monkey jumped back and forth. Soon the men started pulling snakes out of the baskets and boxes in front of them. As their small audience aahed and shrieked, the men handled these creatures with steely indifference. One began playing a short flutelike instrument. (The song is exactly like the one you're now hearing in your head.) On the other end sat a man with leathery skin that contrasted with his striking silver hair and beard. He could not have looked more the part had he been sent from Hollywood.

He was the main attraction.

I began to move slowly from our side of the proceedings to nudge closer, around to his side and then behind him, looking over his shoulder. A small python draped around his neck. I was just four feet away. Everyone on the other side was now laughing (admittedly one of my goals). He knowingly looked up at me with a half smile and a wink. He then motioned for me to sit next to him.

I did.

He put one, then two snakes around my neck. More laughs.

Then he took the lid off the basket.

For the first time (let's go ahead and say the only time) in my life, I saw a cobra rising up out of that basket. Eighteen inches from my leg.

Has time ever slowed for you to see and hear many things

all at once? In that instant, I could not take my eyes off this creature with its hood flaring. The flute fella was still playing that song. The old guy next to me was still whispering and muttering things and occasionally smiling.

There are several things I will not soon forget—that hissing sound as the snake began to sway in front of me, the dread of seeing that hood flare open. I remember the charmer scooting it even closer to me and the immediate message my brain was telling my legs: *Everything about this is wrong; will you please help this fool to scoot back? It is time for the many parts to work as one. Now.*

But mostly I'll remember the eyes. I'd never really paid attention to the eyes of a cobra. I'd never been close enough to notice. I'd never had one looking right at me. The eyes were bluish. I was told later that this was because he was getting ready to start shedding his skin. I don't really know. We didn't stay in touch. I just know my insides were screaming when I came face-to-face with that cobra.

That was an interesting moment. But I'm not sure I'd recommend it. In fact, as a public service to the rest of you, allow me to warn you now and suggest a few ways to avoid such an experience if it ever presents itself to you.

And in some ways, it will.

A BAD NEIGHBORHOOD

We haven't mentioned a particular word group yet, but it gets much attention in Scripture. The practice of it is as deadly as they come to churches, teams, businesses, and individuals. What is it? I'll give you a hint:

It's easier to talk about someone than to him or her.

There are many different words used to describe this behavior: slanderers, babblers, busybodies, gossips. In case you're wondering, none of these is positive. The Old Testament says to not associate with gossips.[1] The New Testament condemns "busybodies" who speak about things they shouldn't.[2] And then there's that list in Romans 1:

> They have become filled with every kind of
> wickedness, evil, greed and depravity. They are full
> of envy, murder, strife, deceit and malice. They are
> gossips, slanderers, God-haters, insolent, arrogant
> and boastful; they invent ways of doing evil.[3]

It keeps going. This is a terribly uncomfortable and convicting list that describes what happens when people refuse to acknowledge God or allow him to work in their lives. And right in the middle are gossips and slanderers. This is not exactly a good neighborhood, but it's where those words (and people) live.

The word we read as *gossip* is sometimes translated *whisperer*, and for good reason. In the Greek it is what your English teacher used to call an onomatopoeia. It is a word that sounds like what it represents. Such as *fizz* or *boom* in our language. It is the word *psithuristés*, which really should be almost whispered, for this is a whisssssperer. The root of this word also meant the whisperings of a snake charmer to his snakes. *Pssssithurissssstesss.*[4]

Why is it we don't pick up on the danger of *psithuristés*? We dismiss it as nothing because it is no louder than a whisper—but it lands on that list between murderers and God haters. It is just plain wrong. It is dangerous to you and me and the person we're talking about. It is dirty and slimy and way creepier than staring at a cobra. If only we could fully appreciate what this does to our souls and to our community and how it breaks the heart of God.

So here's your public service announcement:

If you are close enough to see the color of a cobra's eyes, you are too close.

Let us be wary: This seductive and subtle scheme was born in the mind of the serpent himself. The cowardly whisper of *psst* is more than a silly habit. It is deadly. And its practice indicates an unhealthy, unsafe community.

It's time for us to intentionally deprive it of the ability to thrive in our midst. Protecting the body from such poison will require wisdom and courage and consistency on our part.

For starters, let's look at a few (hopefully) practical thoughts that will protect you.

Beware of Christianese

All teams, businesses, and families have a language. These are the catchphrases and shortcuts known mostly to insiders. Christians have a language too. Assuming you are part of a local church, it, too, will have a language. Hang around for long enough and you'll learn some of the buzzwords and phrases. Hang around certain people and you'll also learn one of the slickest and ickiest form of communication among Christians. If you know this language, you can tuck in a sneaky put-down or juicy update on someone's situation:

- It may come dressed as a godly concern. "You haven't heard? Well, you can just imagine how heartbroken I was to learn that . . ."

- It may come as request to just listen. "Who else could I tell but you, dear brother (or sister) . . ."
- It may come as an invitation to prayer. "Join me, won't you, in praying for that church? I don't know if you've heard, but they just . . ."

In the above examples, the immediate payoff comes when the other person raises an eyebrow upon hearing the news. His or her lips purse together in faux concern. Now both of you are playing along. And both of you can walk away feeling morally superior to whomever. And for the briefest of moments, you are distracted from your own struggles.

But it does no one any good. Ephesians 4:29 puts such talk in its place: "Do not let any unwholesome talk come out of your mouths, but only what is helpful for building others up according to their needs, that it may benefit those who listen." Is the talk that is coming out of that person's mouth "wholesome"? Was that poor soul whose name was just dragged through the mud built up in any way? Did you need that update?

Horrible words wrapped in Christianese are still horrible words.

Talk as Though You're on Speakerphone

An interesting phenomenon of our day is the accidental call placed from your phone. Oftentimes we refer to this as an anatomically assisted dial. (The colloquial term is more picturesque, but I've said enough.) Let's just say that sometimes people unknowingly make a call from their back pocket. I've been told this can happen from within a purse as well. Many of us have received such a call. It's awkward, because you are now essentially eavesdropping on a conversation you innocently tapped into. Still, you really should hang up.

Many have of us have also inadvertently placed that call. When it dawned on you that someone had been listening in, did you play back the conversation in your head to make sure you hadn't said anything ugly or embarrassing?

Or there's this variation on a theme: Have you ever gone too far with your words and then looked down at your phone—*just to make sure it was off*?

Phew.

I've heard well-intentioned people suggest that things would be far different if we imagined ourselves speaking all our words in front of Jesus. And that makes sense. That should matter. But apparently it doesn't. Apparently we forget our lives *are* lived before, as Hagar said, "the God who sees me."[5] Gulp.

Until that comforting and convicting thought sinks in, try this: Take the split-second dread that you'd been found out by your friend and pull it forward—right *before you say those words in the first place*. Are these just mind games? Maybe not. Think of it as a way to establish a new habit. For just a week, a month, or a year, imagine that person listening in when you speak of him or her. What if you were on speakerphone for the whole team or small group or neighborhood to hear? How would your words be different? It is an interesting little exercise, that one.

Question Others

What you just told me—is that true? How do you know this to be true? Where did you hear such things?

You will rarely get answers to these questions, but their

mere presence will throw a wet blanket on the sparks of this potential wildfire. So much of what we whisper to others is half-heard, half-baked, half-true. Like children participating in a party game, we murmur an already distorted story in someone's ear, and it only gains more inaccuracies as it's passed down the gossip network. At each stop, this "true story" leaves more hurt and dissension, picking up steam along the way. We are so prone to believe the worst possible explanation that it will not take much for trouble to brew. The perverse person of Proverbs 16:28 stirs things up. This is what happens. Things are stirred up—true, half-true, or not at all true. But now there is dissension. Do not give it a chance.

What do you expect me to do with this?

Now we are back to something rotten wrapped in churchy language. Were you even supposed to be invited into this impromptu prayer meeting? Proverbs 11:13 says that "a gossip betrays a confidence." Is that what just happened? Was a problem, an embarrassment, or a struggle entrusted to someone, only to have him or her put that private pain on display?

Why did you tell me this?

Perhaps the motives are less slimy than I'm suggesting. But Proverbs 16:28 holds a dire warning and a different motive you should know about: "A gossip separates close friends." The harsh truth is that some will intentionally try to separate others with their words. Rather than using a meat cleaver, they have developed a surgical precision with the carefully placed whispers. Beware.

Do you feel safe around such people? Well, you shouldn't. Let me explain what they are doing when you are not around: the very same thing that is happening when you are in the room. Why would it be otherwise? In a gossiping culture, no one is safe—including the gossipers. Trust erodes so gradually that people don't even notice when it finally dies.

Do not let it go this far. Throw bright light on these words. Question one another.

And then, with great love and courage, tell someone you are not playing along. Even then, be careful with those words you're using. One of the best ways to work against the wiles of evil is to encourage someone—when appropriate— to go back to the person being talked about. *If you are that concerned, go to that person, but don't let this go any further.*

In healthier cultures, no one is immune to gossip, but there is significant resistance to it. Take some of the perverse pleasure out of the "psst," and it will decrease. But this is something that must be taught, talked about, and lived out. And then when any one of us slips—and we will—it must be addressed *as soon as you are made aware*. Always be ready to offer grace. Do you see how all of this fits together? We're not shocked by one another's mistakes, but we will not allow them a foothold.

When the grace-restored are the grace-ready, there is a chance. There is hope. And this new way—though never perfect—will produce a culture that starts to reject the old ways. It's quite possible that those who refuse to learn this new, better way will simply grow tired and move on.

For many reasons, questioning one another in loving but direct ways is a good thing.

Question Yourself

That just doesn't look right, does it? So often we are told in our world to never question ourselves. *Go for it. It's your life—live it.* But when it comes to resisting the devil as he uses one of his favorite tricks, it's entirely reasonable to question yourself before you go any further with that new information.

Ask yourself: *What was my first reaction to the news?*

Be honest here. Bracingly honest. What was your first thought after hearing this information? *I knew it?* Followed by a slight but undeniable smirk? An unholy gloat? You may be aware of the strange but telling word *Schadenfreude.* It's a German word that comes from the combination of two words: *Schaden,* meaning "damage" or "harm," and *Freude,* meaning "joy." *Harm-joy*—that's the word. It is the enjoyment derived from seeing or hearing about someone else's troubles.

What an ugly, accurate word. We humans derive smirky joy from hearing about someone else's struggles. When such a person has threatened our own unstable self-worth, news of his or her stumbling is a source of self-righteous glee. We would never admit it out loud, but what we just heard was schadenfreudtastic.[6]

That is not a good sign, and it leads to the next, related question:

Am I secretly rooting for that person's failure?

Our tolerance for these reports from the underbelly of someone's life is often connected to an odd competitiveness with that person. Secretly we envy the attention he or she receives. We grow to resent his or her success. Why has God blessed his or her business or ministry so? At this point, discovering the truth is not even a priority. We are eager to believe the worst because it will make it easier to root against that individual. If you do not wish to see this person succeed, then these words are as lethal as they come.

Am I already thinking of whom I will tell?

More than any other question to ask ourselves, this may be the most diagnostic. When we hear sad or shocking words, our thoughts—if left unchecked by the Spirit—might run to who "needs" to know this information. If we apply the above questions to that moment, it is likely no one "needs" to know.

When you or I start imagining how people are going to fall out of their chairs when they hear this—we have just revealed the true nature of our heart on this matter. We are all too eager to drop this little bombshell.

This is gossip, and it must stop.

If you are close enough to see the color of a cobra's eyes, you are too close.

Let's kill this thing every time it rises in front of us with its hood flared, hissing the whisper of a secret. We can no longer tolerate gossip as a lesser sin on that disturbing list in Romans 1.

Our new way of working together will not only be marked by the absence of whispery gossip. For every warning in Scripture, there is a promise of what good and godly words can accomplish. So why don't we end this chapter on a good note? (Yes, please.)

A DIFFERENT KIND OF WHISPER

Spend your good words extravagantly. Sprinkle them generously into conversations. Remember, they have the power of life and death. To repeat: *They have the power of life.* So stand with people and beside them, and when they are not in the room, stand for them. And on those days you stand beside them, watch for moments when you and only you will be able to speak from a place rooted in your own struggle. From there, you and only you will be able to speak strong words of God's faithfulness. It is the prayer prayed close. It is a quiet but strong word that only a few will hear. It is a different kind of whisper.

Our church is involved with an initiative by Living Water International to mobilize and connect churches to one another—in places around the world and the United States. Because our particular focus is in the country of Zimbabwe, we eagerly hosted two influential leaders in the vast network of churches there. We hoped this would be an opportunity to encourage their very important work in a country still sitting on a knife's edge.

As it turns out, it was a chance for them to do the same for us.

In the course of their time here, they met with young pastors we are mentoring throughout our city. One of those meetings was with a young African American pastor who serves with grace and courage in a difficult situation. Two of our pastors came back from that private meeting with tears in their eyes. "I wish you could've heard the words they quietly spoke to Andre."

These visiting leaders know what it is to minister in the ruins of a neighborhood that was once something else. They know what it is to long for God to do a new work. They know about self-doubt and discouragement. They know about racial strife and outright conflict that has left scars on all sides—for this is Zimbabwe. They know what it is to pray for miracles, and they know what it is to hope, for God is doing something in their midst.

These quiet, fervent prayers of elder statesmen, prayed over a young pastor who lives halfway around the world, will make the difference. The strong words spoken quietly breathed life. They kept telling him—barely above a whisper—that he was not alone. God was with him—and so were they. They told him he was not crazy for praying bold prayers and dreaming big dreams.

When no one else was around, they spoke words that came from someplace personal, and those words went straight to the soul of a pastor God will use to change the world.

With our mouths we can boast, curse, or poison. Or we can bring life, hope, and healing. Do not underestimate how powerfully damaging your words can be to others. As a public service, let's stay away from those situations where we can do damage. It is more dangerous than we can imagine.

But oh, the potential of your words to further the Kingdom! You may never give a sermon, and that's just fine. The world probably doesn't need another sermon anyway. But your words mean everything to the Kingdom. Sometimes you will shout to the world of your faith. But more often than not, what makes a difference will be that whisper of a different kind to someone who wants to give up. You will breathe life into a soul: "You're not crazy for caring that much." "I'm not going anywhere." "You are not alone."

But to whisper those words to another, you will need to be close.

FOR REFLECTION AND DISCUSSION

Why is gossip so destructive?

How would the "speakerphone" principle affect your conversations?

Why is the "different kind of whisper" so important?

How can you use your words to "breathe life" into the people around you?

10

HANG ON TO THAT RED SHIRT

Entering the Trouble of Another

"Praise be to the God and Father of our Lord Jesus Christ, the Father of compassion and the God of all comfort, who comforts us in all of our troubles."[1] These are the opening lines of another letter written by Paul, and he wastes no time. He's just getting warmed up, and already we are in the deep end of the pool. Way to go, Paul—great opener. You might even say it was inspired.

But be honest. Which word stuck out? Depending on the week you've had (and we've all had them), it might've been this one:

Troubles.

Just in case you're unfamiliar with the concept, the word translated *trouble* or *affliction* means "pressed down."[2] The root of that word goes back to the pressing of grapes. The winepress of the ancient world involved workers stepping into a trough filled with grapes, which they would proceed to stomp, squeezing the grape juice out. Perhaps you've seen this done. The fact that it is no longer widely practiced is an improvement. I for one am not interested in any food product resulting from direct contact with a stranger's bare foot. But that was how it worked back then.

The word could also refer to a well-worn path where the grass gets trampled into dirt. Either way, the imagery works and we are ready for the next question. Do you know what it feels like to be stepped on, pushed down, or worn thin by something over and over? In a world with over seven billion stories, the size and shape of that foot will vary, but most of us are familiar with a trouble that stomps and squeezes the seeming life out of us.

Speaking of openings, this one turned out to be quite the pick-me-upper.

So there's trouble. That's not great news, but it's not breaking news either. What makes this the beginning of a very big thought for us is how the words *comfort* and *trouble* are mentioned in the same breath—as if this really happens. Paul is telling this church that they worship *the God of all comfort.*

Because he knows.

WHY SOME SING THE WAY THEY DO

Have you ever been in a church where the great hymns are sung? Have you ever listened to the singing around you swell into an outcry of faith mingled with defiance? Not of God, but a defiance of the trouble that has tried to stomp the life out of those worshipers? Listen carefully. The tones are coming from someplace deep now, the voices more raw than reverent.

When sorrows like sea billows roll
Whatever my lot, thou hast taught me to say
It is well, it is well with my soul.[3]

How are some able to sing such things in the face of troubles that are crashing over the sides?

Because they know.

Notice that Paul doesn't say God swoops in and rescues us immediately, though that sounds wonderful. Our Creator doesn't offer us a cheat code so we can bust out of this part of life. There is no secret escape hatch. The trustworthy Scriptures promise instead that God is there with us, comforting us *in* all our troubles. Yes, he can and often does rescue us *from* trouble. So we pray for those moments.

But in the waiting weighed down with worry, God is also there. In the fear, God is there. In the creeping sadness, God is there—comforting us in all our trouble. And yet that doesn't sound like enough. This is in part because our word *comfort* has been bled of its strength. Comfort is what happens when the air-conditioning works or the chair is soft. Comfort is a patronizing "there, there" pat on the back after you skinned your knee. This, however, does not approach the comfort God is offering.

In addition to being translated as "comfort," the word *parakaleo* can mean to "call alongside"—as in "walk with me" or "don't try this alone."[4] It is to encourage, even to lovingly challenge someone. The more familiar noun form *paraclete* is the word Jesus uses for the Holy Spirit. This, we learn from other Scripture passages, is the work of the Holy Spirit. This is what God offers to those in trouble. He calls you to his side in the middle of the trial, not just afterward.

Dallas Willard said it precisely: "God's presence is the whole story. *This interaction between us and the God who is present with us always is what the resurrection is really about.* . . . [It] isn't just that Jesus won; *it's that he is now living with us.*"[5] The presence of God will sustain us and see us through.

This is why some sing the way they do.

OUR NEED FOR THE TANGIBLE

But still, others will wonder if this isn't all too subjective. If God's presence is "the whole story," we don't want to miss it. Especially when facing trouble of our own. This leads to a rather blunt admission that, as a pastor, I've heard more than once: "I do pray and I do find peace in that. I will cling to those Scriptures. But right now I need something tangible." What people want is something physical. It reminds me of the oft-told story[6] of a little boy who was afraid to be in his room alone at night, in the dark. Eventually, his father tried to console him with deep, biblical truth: "Just go back to sleep . . . God is with you." To which the little boy replied, "But I want somebody with skin on!"

Cute story.

But it offers a clue for us in how this comforting sometimes works. Ours is a life of faith. It is beyond the reassurance of what I can see with my own eyes and touch with my own hands, this life with God. Jesus said as much to Thomas after they cleared the air a week after the Resurrection.[7] To personally interact with the God who does not fit in the dimensions of our universe will be like no other relationship. We should expect this. But God in his infinite mercy is not offended by our need for the tangible. It is, in fact, one of the ways he will comfort us in our troubles.

But first, a word or two about a word.

BODY LANGUAGE

Incarnation. It doesn't even make it into our Bibles, but it describes a truth so essential to our faith. It is the miracle that describes the unique life of Jesus. As J. I. Packer has said, "Nothing in fiction is so fantastic as is this truth of the Incarnation."[8]

The Word—this one who was there at the beginning of all things, who was with the creator God, and somehow is God—found a way to squeeze into a finite, physical form. The inestimable Eugene Peterson phrased it as such in *The Message*: "The Word became flesh and blood, and moved into the neighborhood."[9] You want something tangible? The eternal Son walked the planet as one of us. The rest of that Gospel is John telling us what it was like following his friend and teacher, who just happened to be the King of the universe. "I was there," John says. *We have seen his glory.*

But as a disciple in those glory-saturated days, John also saw Jesus get tired and thirsty like everyone else. He saw him hurt and disappointed. He saw him laugh and get upset and weep openly. Jesus' feet got dirty (and no doubt stank), and his hands were callused before they were forever scarred. Nothing in fiction compares to what really happened.

And always layered beneath the story of the Cross is the wonder of the Incarnation.

At Christmas, Easter, and Communion we remember the fantastically real story of the Incarnation. This is right and good—and yet there is more. If we only look over our shoulders at a sliver of time in first-century Palestine when God the Son walked among us, we are missing what is still possible in front of us.

What if there were some aspects of the Incarnation—God being in the world in a physical, flesh-and-blood way—that applied to us? Quickly comes now the warning against heresy, for God's plan was never for us to become gods in our own right. The answer does not come from within. How silly and seductive this reasoning goes: Once I discover my full potential, life and the world will be as it should be. (I would think by now we've got plenty of data collected on how that one isn't working out.) We are not gods. We desperately need help—a Savior, if you will. And he has come to us. This is the very good news of the gospel.

But this same Savior says to his followers, "As the Father has sent me, I am sending you."[10] Not to be saviors, of course. But God will work through us in this world, in part, the way he worked through Jesus. How? With our physical presence, we the rescued ones will not just tell people who Jesus is but give them a sense of who he is. One more time: You can't do this on your own. Augustine writes, "Indeed we also work, but we are only collaborating with God who works, for his mercy has gone before us"—and then the famous punch line—"for without him we can do nothing."[11] We will need God's help, but we are to show up in the trouble of this world. Reggie McNeal assures us that God will do the heavy lifting,[12] but still we have to show up.

With the Spirit's presence in us, we are the body of

Christ in a more literal sense than some first imagined. Talk about fantastic. Three chapters later, Paul talks about the very life of Jesus being revealed in his mortal (flesh and blood) body.[13] As one noted pastor once put it, "The church is his body; it is the physical form of his presence on earth. Touch the church and you touch the body of Christ, which means you touch Christ."[14]

That also means that when the body of Christ touches the world, so too does Jesus.

It is one of the ways he comforts people in their troubles.

ENTERING THE CHAOS

In the waking nightmare of death and political dead ends that is now Syria, the rest of the world watches in horror. But we are too interconnected to watch from a distance. Hate that ferments in one region of the world now easily erupts in another. This is trouble with a capital *T*. Lost in the morass are the millions displaced by these conflicts, the vast majority of whom only want to return home. In fact, almost all of them will show you their house keys—for they locked things up when they fled persecution and are desperate go home, to what I can't imagine.

Until then, millions of refugees hover at the borders of their homeland, waiting. Wondering. Barely existing. Spending time in Beirut with Christians willing to touch this part of the world is humbling. Sitting in a plastic tent just minutes from the Syrian border is unsettling. A desperate mother sits in a tent worrying how she will provide for and protect her five daughters with her husband missing. Her daughters are desperate too. As Michael Gerson, sitting in that same tent with me, wrote of the daughters in a *Washington Post* column, "The oldest, Batoul, 13, has written out a letter in neat Arabic. 'I miss you dad,' it says. 'I feel like I'm choking when I tell my story because it ends with you not next to me.'"[15] The stories and details change from family to family but not by much. The pervasive feeling is hopelessness. Dignity has been eviscerated. Families split apart. Children traumatized.

This is what it means to be in trouble.

And yet to walk the camps with Rich Stearns (our host), president of World Vision, I couldn't help but realize the need for Jesus to show up in a tangible way. This is a crisis for our generation, the scale of which we may be afraid to take in. But we must. Again, in the words of Mike Gerson, "If American churches and charities are not relevant here, they are irrelevant."[16]

But we *can* be relevant, and Jesus does show up there. This is how it happens: Relief organizations such as World Vision have the opportunity to enter these chaotic places in ways the rest of us won't. As we who follow Jesus partner with them, we are working together as one. But it is not just the aid that is brought by such groups, needed as that may be. It is the physical presence that does more than we first imagine. I saw this point well made by Rich and the World Vision folks in the region. It was and is a calling to come alongside: *You're not forgotten. We are not going anywhere. Let's walk together.*

In a tangible way, the followers of Jesus have entered the chaos, moving closer to the trouble, not farther away. This is the story of the Incarnation.

It is one of the ways God comforts people in their troubles—with a flesh-and-blood presence. And now it's our turn. No, most of us aren't heading to any of the world's hot zones. But we don't have to travel that far to find affliction.

For you know someone in trouble. And perhaps that person is you.

PRAYERS FROM AN INDIAN TRAIN STATION

A few years ago I was privileged to take my family with me on one of those trips to India. India is like few places on Earth, a cacophony of beauty and struggle. The sounds, colors, and smells are like a wondrous wave. Add to that the beauty of its people and the power of the one true God at work in this land, and you've got quite the experience. Maybe that's why I keep going back.

But this time, after waving good-bye to the rest of our crew, we stayed—just the four of us—to see some things in India I'd never seen, eat a little more curry, get lost in a billion people, that sort of thing. I thought it would be romantic and relaxing to travel from Delhi to Agra, home of the Taj Mahal. What teenage girl wouldn't want to see this "wonder of the world" with the famous romantic backstory?

We were then to take the train back from Agra to Delhi, but our hosts booked that passage. But not from Agra. From . . . well, let's just call it "NotAgra" instead of using its real name. I'm still not sure how and why this was the plan. Perhaps our hosts thought we'd like the train from NotAgra better.

Getting to that train meant a car ride from Agra. When I asked about travel to this other city by car, I saw the staff at our hotel trade a serious of nervous looks and whispers. The only word I could make out again and again was "NotAgra," followed by another nervous look. "NotAgra? Sir, you cannot be boarding the train there. Surely you did not mean to go to NotAgra."

Now I was nervous.

After a flurry of calls and more looks, we determined there was no room on any other train. They would arrange a driver to take our family to this other station. Upon meeting him we went through the same routine. "NotAgra? Surely you don't mean NotAgra. Why would you have me take you there?"

Now we were all nervous.

But we had a flight back to Delhi late that evening that we had to make. This was our only way out, so our driver took us the ninety minutes or so to NotAgra. Our situation went from "this will be fine" to "please, God" over the course of that drive. At the end of the journey, we found ourselves slowly maneuvering through a massive crowd that peered in through the windows at three beautiful women and one fool of a man. And I'm pretty sure they were all asking the same question. "NotAgra? Surely you did not mean to come to NotAgra."

When the car stopped, the driver instructed me to not get out of the car or unlock it for anyone. He asked for a specific number of rupees and told me to tuck everything else in my boot and to not take that money out again until I was on the train.

And then he left us—to go find a red-shirted porter to help with our luggage and much more. As it turned out, our driver would not be allowed to go any farther with us. So this man he was about to introduce me to would take us through the crowd and to the station, and he would get us on the right train, because none of the signs were in English.

When I say the driver "introduced" us, I mean I shook the porter's hand. Told him the name of the train and where we were going. That was the extent of our conversation because he spoke no English and my Hindi is laughable. He nodded, took my girls' backpacks, and started walking. Our driver smiled and shook my hand. I think I saw a tear in the corner of his eye as he said good-bye—he was concerned about us. We were now surrounded by a mob of curious men, and I had to get these three women through the crowd quickly. I was watching everything. The Bible says to be anxious for nothing but pray about everything.[17] Well, I got half of it right. I was praying about everything *and* anxious about most of it. Very anxious. As you are learning, I've done more than a few crazy things in my life and have invited my kids into a few of them. But nothing compared to this moment. My instructions to them were simple: "Stay close, stay where I can see you, and don't lose sight of that guy wearing the red shirt."

We were tired. It was hot. The train was interminably late. For the first hour or so, I tucked Robin and the girls in a little room with no ventilation, where a sweet woman instantly assessed the situation and kept them close. It is hard to explain, but this situation made others nervous for us, so I figured I'd be nervous too. Oh, and there was no cell coverage. We were on our own and so far from home.

Talk about winning Father of the Year.

I paced along the tracks, praying: *God, it seems to me we're in trouble, and I am so wanting out of it. I don't even know how this happened, but I need you desperately. I can't read the names on these trains, and we cannot spend the night here. Keep these three beautiful women safe, and get us out of this jam.* And of course, he did. But how? How did God walk us out of that trouble?

The man in the red shirt.

Hours later, our train finally came. I gathered through his hurried hand signals that all three of the women should push in right behind him. I knew why. At each stop, there was a mad rush to stuff the train full before it quickly took off again. I gave my wife and the girls the same instructions as before: "Don't take your eyes off the man in the red shirt. Do not get separated from him. I'll be right behind you, but if you have to, *hang on to that red shirt.*"

The train stopped. A surge of humanity crushed in and out of those little cars. The porter stepped on while I watched one girl, then the second, and then Robin climb on. Still pushing. Walking through the car until we reached our own little Harry Potter train cabin. Except it was hot and old and not so magical. But that man dropped our bags and looked me in the eyes with just a little hint of a smile before he received the biggest tip I've ever given anyone. He knew he'd done it. He'd walked us through that chaos and out of trouble.

THE ANSWER TO YOUR PRAYER

There will be times in your life when you can't even tell which way to go—the grief or the shame or the worry is so great that you can't even see straight. The conflict is so loud and the trouble is so chaotic that you just can't seem to find your way out of the mess. And you're going to beg God to show up. You'll ask him what I did—to please show you a way out. And he will. God always answers that prayer. But do you know how?

How he does this is as varied as the size and shape of that

powerful foot squishing us. We bumble our way through his Word and find passages that are custom-fit for our hearts. We pray those passages when we can't find our own words. And then sometimes all we can do is groan, so stepped on are we. But the Spirit of God is there with us, offering courage, comfort, and a peace that laps right up to the edges of our troubled hearts. Yes, this can happen. But God is also going to do something tangible and physical—flesh and blood even for you. He does it for me.

God is going to put someone in your life.

It could be a friend or mentor or pastor or counselor or neighbor. You will hear their voice and see their face and reach out and touch their hand sometimes. God is inviting you to walk with them for a while. They won't have all the answers, but they could be the one friend who is going to love you enough to tell you the truth. They might be the only one there to encourage you when no one else even notices. But let them walk with you now. That is God answering your prayer.

It's almost as if he showed up in a flesh-and-blood sort of way.

SOMEONE WITH SKIN ON

We will not have the same experiences, trials, or troubles. This has the potential to keep us isolated in our various struggles. We figure no one anywhere could possibly understand what's happening to us.

No, we don't have the same troubles, but we know what it is to feel pressed upon, worn down, and stepped upon. And some of us, God be praised, also have some sense of what it means to be comforted by him. The genius of God is this: *We are to share what we've gone through with one another.* This is how we encourage one another. This is how we embody the very presence of the God of all comfort.

We are again in the mystery. But God will use the pain that left a scar on one's heart to now strengthen another. Hope flows ever so slowly from one to the other. And yet God pours comfort in both directions. Now the one with older, partially healed wounds finds meaning in what happened all those years ago. Not a reason—but now something redemptive is finally happening. For the one in the swirling chaos, the other voice will be the only one they hear that day.

And now the rest of the verse: He is "the God of all comfort, who comforts us in all our troubles, so that we can comfort those in any trouble with the comfort we ourselves receive from God."[18]

This is how it works. This is how God sometimes keeps our world from going full tilt over the edge. This is often how he comforts and sustains us. He sends in someone with skin on. Someone who's been through a storm or two. Someone who has experienced his comfort. Someone we can see and hear and hang on to ourselves.

And that makes it, well, incarnational.

It could be your turn. God might be sending you into the hurt. It's your time to call someone alongside you. Along the way you pray, cry, laugh, listen, and remind that other person of God's faithfulness because you know. You whisper and sometimes shout over the chaos . . . but always you remember what it was like when God walked you through your trouble.

If you're in the middle of the trouble, keep your eyes on

Jesus. There's not one person in this world who can offer you what Jesus does. Follow him through the trouble. This is the only way you'll ever sing from someplace deep, "It is well with my soul." But this God who loves you so will comfort you in ways you could never fully put into words. And he may put a person in your life. This person may not be wearing a red shirt but might as well be. He or she will come alongside you and remind you that you are not alone, that this is not the end; he or she will love and serve and encourage and challenge you—and God will be right there, whispering and sometimes shouting through that life. *He is the God of all comfort who comforts us in all our troubles* . . . and this is how he often does it.

Hang on to that red shirt.

FOR REFLECTION AND DISCUSSION

Whom in your life is God calling you to "struggle alongside?"

Whom do you call when the trials of life hit? Have you made yourself available for others to call you?

Why is it important for Jesus followers to "enter the chaos" of their communities?

How is your local church embodying the Incarnation? What steps can you take to get involved with that activity?

11

THE JESUS ANSWER

Lessons Learned in Ferguson

THE SETTING COULDN'T HAVE BEEN MORE PEACEFUL as I stood on a deck overlooking a lake surrounded by rolling, wooded hills. The heat of the day had not yet overtaken the coolness of the morning. But even in the peacefulness, *peace* was not the word that came to my mind. This Saturday in July of 2016 marked the end of a long and violent week in our country. A major news website led with this headline: "Who Can Heal America?"[1]

Few would contest that America needs healing. The tattered nerves of a nation have been fully exposed in recent years. The opening sentence of the article captured this acute pain:

> Raw racial tensions, live-streamed killings, strained trust between the police and communities they serve, and a presidential race that has scorched deep divides have the nation on edge and wondering if a leader will emerge from the chaos.[2]

As I read that article, we were facing an upcoming election. But I am convinced that no matter when you're reading these words, America (and the rest of the world) will still need healing. So the question, with its implied despair, remains. Who *can* heal America? Is there anyone?

No.

That is, if we're talking about any of us.

You know where this is heading. You read the chapter title. You're smart like that. We Christians "know" what the answer is supposed to be. For us, the answer is always Jesus. And yet, we hesitate—because how does that work in the real world? The thought many of us have these days is one we won't admit out loud: *I have no idea how the "Jesus answer" applies here.*

It's true that answering the question with Jesus is obvious. But that doesn't make the answer *any less true*. Nor does it make it Christianly naive. We who live in the United States will not see our country's hurts healed because of America's collective Christian faith. If ever that was a reality, it is no longer. Law scholar John Inazu eloquently explains in his book that we Christians now live in a pluralistic society of many faiths and viewpoints.[3] Now, that doesn't mean we should simply lay down our Scripture-rooted convictions. Rather, we must grapple with what it means to live out our faith in this reality. David Kinnaman and Gabe Lyons's recent work *Good Faith* is a thought-provoking call to do just that. They end a chapter entitled "Who Will Lead?" with these words: "Solving these problems is up to good faith Christians, starting with how we engage our neighbors with whom we disagree."[4]

This is no doubt a significant way in which twenty-first-century Christ followers will have a lasting impact on their world: engaging neighbors with whom they disagree. It is my assertion that how we face the great issues of our day is also inextricably tied to how we Christians engage each other—*especially when we disagree.*

I believe this is where the Jesus answer comes into full view.

Or at least, it should. If only we knew where to start.

A FRAMEWORK MIGHT HELP

Many believers are perplexed and often hesitant. In the midst of this confusion are Christian leaders themselves. We pastors, priests, and ministers are often ill-equipped to deal with our own emotions, much less to help our congregations articulate the hurt and outrage they are experiencing. Our steps are wobbly and our words unsure, and in this way we are no different from the world around us. But such uncertainty is not new.

We've long lived in a society steeped in what one expert has termed "chronic anxiety."[5] Rabbi and family therapist Edwin Friedman tells us that this anxiety is "deeper and more embracing than community nervousness. Rather than something that resides within the psyche of each one, it is something that can envelop, if not actually connect, people."[6]

This anxiety has enveloped us. It has also connected us. For all our differences, we have this in common: We live on the razor's edge. The disquiet in our hearts keeps us hyper-vigilant. Our margins stay narrow, our fuses short. We do not trust those who might look, think, or vote differently from us. We are not sure what we can say—at parties, Bible studies, work, or school. We watch the news, hear a story, read a posting. We see something with our own eyes. And deep inside is the roiling, boiling sense that things are not right.

Where do we start?

Friedman's point of reference was the work of Murray Bowen, a pioneer in family therapy.[7] In dealing with families awash with chronic anxiety, Bowen noticed similar behaviors in larger people groups—including entire societies that had been overwhelmed with anxiety. Could it be that at this time in our history, on this page of our story, our society is much like an overwrought and overmatched family? Not sure of the next move, anxiously swinging back and forth between giving up and lashing out.

Unfortunately, we Christians are no different from the world around us.

And yet we are.

It is our time to shine some light onto the path. It will not be easy or automatic. Nor will everyone join us. Not yet. As Jesus told a teacher of Israel, some people love darkness because what they are doing is evil.[8] And evil hates the light. But it is now time for us to lead with more confidence. Where do we start?

A framework might help.

Let's consider the Jesus answer for this question composed of three interconnected parts. Some of you will now be tempted to dismiss this as too simple. Perhaps, but simple is not a bad place to start when you're feeling overwhelmed.

I warn you: These are not new thoughts, and this is not a comprehensive plan. It's merely a starting point. Hopefully others will elaborate on this, improve upon it, correct what needs correcting, deepen its substance, and broaden its scope.

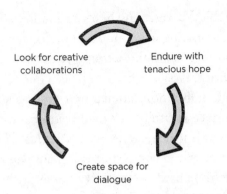

Look for creative collaborations

Endure with tenacious hope

Create space for dialogue

A FRAMEWORK FOR CONSTRUCTIVE CONVERSATION

Here, then, are the three parts of the Jesus answer: A beginning, a middle, and an end (sort of).

One won't work without the other because each supports and fuels the other two. This is not a rigid formula but a framework. Keep your eye on all three. It will require everything we've learned up to now:

1. Create the space for dialogue that won't happen elsewhere.
2. Look for creative collaborations that won't happen elsewhere.
3. Endure with a tenacious hope that isn't found elsewhere.

I warned you they weren't earth shattering.

1. Create Space for Dialogue That Won't Happen Elsewhere

Many conversations taking place in the public square are no doubt having an effect, but most can only go so far before breaking down. People have run out of patience. They have also run out of words—at least the good ones. In the rubble of our own Babel, we keep shouting louder and louder in languages that the people around us no longer understand.

What we're doing is not working.

Should not the people of God have a better chance? Do we not share a common language of grace even when we *do not agree*? We are the people best equipped for difficult dialogue. It will not be easy, but the genius of us working together as one is the way out. It is a tangible expression of how Jesus is the answer. Of course, some of this is already happening in churches and organizations, but it is time for the greater Christian community to intentionally foster these different, better conversations.

Am I the expert now leading the way? Hardly.

I'm just one whom God keeps giving chances to learn from my mistake-ridden journey. And some of what I've learned came from sitting around a table.

In Ferguson, Missouri.

Fellowship Hall

In the summer and fall of 2014, it was Ferguson's turn to grab the world's attention with the shooting death of Michael Brown at the hands of a Ferguson police officer. The details surrounding this event are still shrouded with hurt, high emotion, and a lack of agreement on what actually happened. But on this much all agree: A young man's death sparked a reaction and counterreaction that reached far beyond a small suburb north of St. Louis. It became the all-consuming story of our nation. It also brought to the forefront the topic of systemic oppression and a frustration in the African American community that had remained unseen (or unnoticed) and, from their perspective, unresolved by whites. Add to that a desire for justice (a word used by all), and tension in our city was palpable.

For me, it was a bit more than a national headline. I did not grow up in Ferguson. I would never suggest that I know what it was to feel some of those emotions rushing to the surface of many in those volatile weeks and months.

But I did spend some of the formative years of my life at a church in Ferguson. Some of God's powerful work in drawing me to become a pastor happened in a pew (a pew!) in Ferguson. I have friends who still live and worship there. So I am by no means an expert, but the community, the churches, and the people of Ferguson matter to me personally.

From August to November of that year, and now beyond, our team reached out to pastors—black and white—in that community, asking what we could do to support them and address the issues coming to light. I say "coming to light" as if these were all new developments. What I learned to my own growing conviction is how deep and festering are the hurts of many in our community.

We mostly listened and prayed in the early confusing days. Of course, there are numerous stories of many churches doing the right thing, the good and loving thing, during that time.

For us, much of what we initially learned came from intentional, difficult conversations. In the days leading up to the grand-jury announcement that Officer Wilson would not be prosecuted, and several times after that, we convened off-the-radar meetings. No media would be notified or allowed to attend. The first meeting (and subsequent others) would take place in Ferguson—at the church with those pews. Pastors, law enforcement officers, community organizers, business leaders, a prominent mayor, a chief of police, a state trooper who would oversee operations, and educators from the school districts in the area were invited. One of the pastors in Ferguson, a friend, quietly asked if some of the prominent protestors and the organizers of their movement could attend. Of course. They would be welcomed. Over a dozen others showed up as well.

With that, we all gathered in what this Baptist church calls its "fellowship hall."

Interesting term—*fellowship hall*. Remember, in the streets each night a nervous standoff played out between protestors and law enforcement—and here they were meeting in a church. You could feel the *fellowship* draining right out of that *hall*. Against a backdrop of hurt, anger, and fear and with absolutely no agreement over what happened one afternoon in August, our meeting began.

Around a table.

It wasn't much to look at—a series of long banquet tables forming a large, open square. But we wanted to be around a table.

Scot McKnight says, "Tables create societies."[9] I believe he's right. They're places of meeting. Of convening. Of relationships. He goes on to talk about the importance of an actual physical object to "create space for the invasion of grace."[10] Right again. There's something about sitting around a table that anchors us. We see one another's eyes; we hear one another's voices.

That was the plan, anyway.

It was far from perfect, that first meeting around a table. But it did yield enough results that everyone agreed to come back the next night. Such was the longing for this different kind of place where things could be said and at least heard. The cynic might say our gatherings did no good. The cynic would be wrong. In a few ways I'll share and in many ways I won't, God did something around that table that continues today.

Table Manners

It must be said that the people attending those initial meetings were not all Christians, and some admitted this outright: coming from other faiths or no faith at all. My other clue to this was what I am certain was a new record for instances of a certain word bomb in that fellowship hall. The meeting was—how shall we put this?—raw. But if grace invaded the space around *that* table—and it surely did—then we can create space *anywhere* for our brothers and sisters—with whom we share the Spirit of God—to converse *even when we vehemently disagree.* This is our chance, and it begins with this difficult first step and some things we learned from our first and subsequent talks around a table.

Nobody comes if they aren't asked.

It sounds so obvious. But someone has to make the first awkward move. At first, some will wonder about the details—who's coming? why are they coming? where is the meeting?—and all those things matter. But hold them loosely. Offer to host unless the most loving thing to do would be to allow someone else to host. Pray when you get together, but do more than pray. Our experience has been that in the aftermath of a tragedy, there's a sudden outbreak of prayer meetings. This is such a good thing. But now it is time to talk and listen and learn. Soon we will take action.

None of that can happen unless people are invited.

Do not expect people to say things perfectly.

In fact, expect the opposite. Well-meaning people, speaking from their hearts, are not always (or even usually) eloquent. Nor are they always careful. In previous chapters, we've spoken of the power of words. It all applies here. Pay particular attention if you speak from a position of power. With these conversations will come great passion. With great passion comes the occasional misstep. This will happen. What happens after that often determines how things will go.

Friedman lists certain characteristics of chronically anxious families that might apply here. One is an "intense reactivity."[11] There are no small or slow reactions. Everyone is quick to interpret one another and in the least flattering ways. When this happens in a dialogue—everything shuts down.

But there is another way.

I remember watching an African American pastor smile gently and patiently when someone was less than respectful to one of his suggestions. He did not like or agree with what had just been said. However, it did not end the conversation, for there were bold words he would still speak. But first he created margin in the room for such verbal misfires. Proverbs 19:11 tells us that "it is to one's glory to overlook an offense." That's what I witnessed more than once. This pastor did not ignore the greater issues. In fact, it was because of those issues that he would not allow a slighter offense to pull him off focus.

Much of your energy will be spent on listening.

It's hard to hear things from a different perspective. But remember how taxing it is for the other person to explain (again) life through his or her eyes. The first reaction to hearing another's perspective—especially when part of the problem comes your way—will be what Friedman calls a displacement of blame.[12] You're convinced that this can't be what you or "your side" did wrong. While someone is speaking, you start immediately building an argument against that notion. Unfortunately, you are no longer listening—you are defending or deflecting or debunking or maybe some other word that starts with a *d*—but you are not listening.

But you must if there's any chance of moving forward.

I witnessed that highly visible chief of police listen to an angry protestor about something very specific that was happening on the streets. He wrote down the details. Winced at least once but heard every word. His answer was simple and straightforward: "You're right. That was wrong. I'll make sure it doesn't happen again." It didn't solve everything. But he listened. He admitted someone else was right and vowed to take action. Pile up enough of those moments and you might have something.

You're already contagious. Use it to your advantage.
Eye rolls, half-muttered put-downs, and sarcastic laughter travel faster than the plague around a table. Such is the result of being close. Now use it to your advantage. "A harsh word stirs up anger," we read in Proverbs 15, but don't forget the front half of the verse: "A gentle answer turns away wrath."[13] I saw the gentle voice of a young protester and the kind tone of a pastor turn the volume down at different times. As you pray constantly in those moments, may it be your nonanxious, grace-filled response that is contagious.

Speak truth to your "herd."

Friedman warns us about what he calls "herding." In a herd, no one is really allowed to have their own opinion, and problems are usually lumped into all-or-nothing categories. It becomes increasingly difficult to "even see things differently from the rest of the 'herd.'"[14]

There will come moments when we must break from whatever herd we think we belong to and speak truth because it is truth. Christians—on all sides of a debate—need to say some things out loud that others in their herd will not say. Far too many people I know are afraid of losing a debate. So they remain silent when they are the ones who could speak powerfully.

We the people of God will not agree on all matters or on how to best address every matter. Particularly when the hurts run so deep and the wounds are continually reopened. But for us to have different conversations than the rest of the world, we must stand against evil as it is exposed and admit the truth whenever it shows up. Even when it doesn't align with our original position, gut feeling, or political persuasion.

One writer put it like this: "Be humble enough to highlight truth and virtue on the other side—and to criticize wrongdoing on your own side."[15] (I don't like using the language of "sides," but such is our fractured world.) Truth is spoken across the table and to our "side." It is never aimed like a heat-seeking missile. But such moments of humility and courage slowly build trust around the table.

So too does a very simple act.

Distance Demonizes

Many leaders I reached out to helped shape and inform our actions in those days of 2014 and beyond. Among them was a dear friend, a pastor in Baltimore, David Anderson. David sometimes speaks at our church, and I have spoken at his. As we watched the events unfold, we talked openly. We shared our hearts. I asked him bluntly to help me understand the perspective of an African American male in twenty-first-century America because I am—I believe the technical term is—*white*.

We talked, we prayed, we kidded each other, and we wept and dreamed of how God alone could heal these hurts that run so deep. I also asked David—an expert in racial reconciliation—to co-lead those initial meetings in Ferguson. We could write an entire book about our experiences in those hours. But for the sake of privacy (and my editor), let me tell you the biggest lesson I learned from our time around the table. It will be good to remember this truth as we move from the beginning to the middle of the Jesus answer.

Distance demonizes.

David told all of us an African proverb to illustrate this point. It is found at the end of his very helpful book *Gracism*:

> *When I saw him from afar, I thought he was a monster.*
> *When he got closer, I thought he was just an animal.*
> *When he got closer, I recognized that he was a human.*
> *When we were face to face, I realized that he was my brother.*[16]

Distance demonizes. From a distance it's easier to treat you as a threat, an enemy, a monster. But when the gap is closed, I see a person—with your own story. Your own family. Your own concerns. You are "you" and not an "it."

In that first meeting, some protestors recognized one of the lead officers who was on the streets most nights. He recognized them as well. Even if the memories were vague, a photograph had captured at least one encounter. The photo had been picked up by some of the news services. It showed a young woman screaming into the face of a steely-eyed police officer. It spoke volumes.

You can see the desperate outrage. Her job that night? To protest.

You can also see the firm resolve. His job that night? To protect.

Both were doing exactly what they thought needed to be done.

You can argue that there was a better way for each of them to go about their business, but on this night they sat at the same table. Soon a sheepish awareness that the other was in the room gave way to genuine dialogue. First about police practices. About what it feels like as an African American to be stopped on the way to work for some vague traffic violation. She told him how the whole system feels rigged against her. She tried to describe a fear and powerlessness he'd just have to believe because he'd never understand it. There was anger about some of the initial tactics used by the police. Nervous laughter peppered the room at times. It is quite a thing to speak directly to power. He mostly listened and occasionally nodded in agreement.

When it was his turn, the officer spoke of his own feelings when a cop anywhere does something criminal and how that cannot be defended or ignored. If it's wrong, then it's wrong. Period. But then he told the room what it feels like when someone screams profane things about him or threatens his family. She mostly listened and occasionally nodded in agreement.

Both admitted in front of all the others things they could do differently. And at least they both caught a glimpse into the other's life. The meeting continued, but at the end, another photo was taken (her idea). This time side by side. Smiling. No screaming. No riot gear. Just people. Not monsters. People.[17]

Was this the magic answer that made it all better? Of course not. But for some people, something changed. This officer and other protest leaders shared phone numbers *so they could text one another in the midst of the protest* in case things deteriorated. They were actually working together for people's safety. Did they still disagree about some things? Yes. Did they find some things on which they could agree? A few. There was (and still is) a humanizing effect that happened around that table. It can stretch further into the future if encouraged and revisited. Not because they agree on everything or even most things. But because a distance was bridged.

If these people can do this in the heat of a tense moment, what is stopping the rest of us?

2. Look for Creative Collaborations That Couldn't Happen Elsewhere

In the middle of the Jesus answer we risk trying something together.

To keep us from merely reacting, we must all feel a sense of progress. And progress means addressing the core reasons and issues for unrest. In an anxious society, Friedman warns of the danger of wanting a quick fix. "Can someone please make this conflict go away?" This can lead to a constant state of dealing with only the latest moment but never fully addressing the real issue. If a room is filling with gas fumes, we of course need to make sure no one strikes a match. But at what point do we open the windows, disperse the fumes, and find the gas leak?[18]

In this stage, we should make a sustained effort to focus on specific issues at the root of these uneasy times. This will take time. In the wake of the Ferguson conversations, we continue to experience haunting remnants and fresh reminders of our nation's struggle with race. Many do not want to hear of this. You may want to move on. So does everyone else. But this complex and checkered narrative deserves a meaningful response. People deserve such a response.

Interestingly, the most powerful conversations have often occurred once we leave the table and take action. The distance continues to close in the side-by-side work. This is where God can heal both blindness and old wounds—one awkward step at a time. But it is in this middle stage that we *do* something. This is why you are standing side by side. Commitments made to one another and a community must now become a tangible investment of money and human capital. As David Anderson notes, "Words matter, but actions make them matter more."[19]

Some of the actions taken need to be with new, unorthodox partnerships in which new ideas are hatched. In the incubator of some of our meetings and relationships of step one, we now consider things not imagined before. All sparked by the Spirit responding to our working as one. These are not clearly marked paths. You will need to improvise along the way. John Paul Lederach tells us, "If we are to invoke the moral imagination, we must incite and excite the artist within us."[20] Some will say we are crazy for trying such things, but we must try them together. We must adjust and learn along the way. But finally we will be taking action beyond another meeting. We still need to keep talking around that table, but finally we will be doing something!

Now we must do something for a long time.

It is in the aftermath of a tragedy, when media trucks have moved on to the next headline, that steps—often small and unimpressive—will lead to lasting change. Over time, the faithfulness of Christians partnering across city and church lines will win the battle.

In the future, you and your surprising partnerships will write this story. And by the way, as you do this, work with motivated partners and people who know how to dream as big as you do. Go where God leads you. But do something together for a long time. For us in Ferguson, this has led to specific efforts in three areas: (1) partnering with school districts around issues of literacy, (2) providing resources to young pastors as they become Kingdom entrepreneurs, and (3) mentoring law enforcement officers. Along the way, God has even shown us how these efforts can intersect.

But we must stay the course. For a long time. For us, we speak of investing for *a generation or two*. That's the long view, and we Christians can see that far.

And then when people tell us we're crazy for believing God can still heal, we will tell them about the *really long view*.

3. Endure with a Tenacious Hope That Cannot Be Found Elsewhere

"Let us not grow weary of doing good, for in due season we will reap, if we do not give up doing good."[21]

People across the conservative-liberal spectrum can agree: Racism is sin. So too is the violence against innocents—no matter their color.

That means we are in a battle between good and evil.

God is calling us to face it all with humble, even broken hearts, but never hopeless ones. Come to the table, to many tables—for meetings, for dinner, for Communion as we celebrate the grace of our Lord, all the while knowing we will gather one day around another table for the supper to end all suppers described in Revelation 19.

And at that table, in that day, there will be no more hurt. No more hatred. No more fear or anger or darkness. No more tears. There will be no more wondering how we are going to coexist.

For we will be home. And we will be healed.

This is how the story ends.

This is our hope.

Until then, we have been called to do things differently: "Turn from evil and do good; seek peace and pursue it."[22] Peace. This is what we long for. This is what we are to pursue. Not merely the absence of conflict, but shalom. We have been taught so well by so many that we know by now that *shalom* is even more than our word *peace*. It is a satisfying wholeness we can barely imagine. This is how things were at the beginning and how they will be again.

May God help us as we pursue this peace. But may he

also give us the courage to confess to one another. I walk on tender ground that some would say is not mine to cover, but may God lead us to forgive. It will cost us, this forgiveness, it always does. Tim Keller gives us that beautiful, honest warning.[23] But this too is part of the Jesus answer. So together we pursue this shalom. This peace. This put-back-togetherness.

In the hard work of the beginning and the middle, we remind one another of the end. We are not crazy for believing that God can really heal this hurt. We are not crazy for believing that some of that healing can happen now. One of the ways we will remind one another of this truth is by telling stories—old and new. In his work around the world as a peacemaker, Lederach has learned the power of such stories. From a Tajik warlord, no less, comes this helpful reminder: "You have to circle into the truth through stories."[24]

So one last story.

AN INSTRUMENT OF PEACE

After long and productive conversations that are leading to action with civic and business leaders and educators, there was another gathering. Around a table.

Without going into great detail, this conversation was between an African American worship leader and a young white officer. Many heartfelt interactions had already taken place around this table: I heard words such as "That should never happen" and "I can't imagine" and then these: "I'm sorry."

No one on either side of that table could fully understand the other side, but the distance was being bridged. It was safe enough now for this young officer to share from an even deeper place—to say that he thought his work was what he was called to do, but it wasn't what he expected, this calling. And then he spoke of the burden that comes from seeing death. A particular accident came to his mind. Tough guy. Honest guy. And here, among his peers, the slightest emotion pooled in his eyes.

That's when Nicki, the young woman, leaned forward to bestow favor on this young man. She reminded him how important his calling is. She thanked him for his courage and integrity. She shared some of what is her burden to carry in this world and then this: "I am so sorry for the weight on your shoulders. I am sorry for what has been said and done to you that is wrong." She had done nothing to this officer, and he knew it. He looked at her and said the same: "I am so sorry for what has happened to you that you never deserved."

And then she sang a well-known prayer: "Lord, make me an instrument of your peace." There it was. Floating over and then filling the room. Peace. This is what I couldn't find that morning on the deck overlooking the lake. Peace. But this is what we pursue together—we broken, grace-soaked people who will not give up. This our hope. That God can do this. When the plan is working and we are making progress. When it isn't and we try again. When someone says something and our hearts fill with anger. When we see something live-streamed that knocks us to our knees. We will pursue peace.

On that same deck at the end of that same horrid summer week, I was privileged to be part of a conference call in which I mostly listened to leaders from across America. There was much wisdom shared—some of which has informed these pages. But at the end, Dr. Gerald Durley was asked to close with his comments and prayer. He spoke of the early days with Dr. King. He reminded us that this was not a new struggle. He told us to not lose hope. He proclaimed the sovereignty of God, and then he said these words: "These things that seem over our heads are still under his care."

God is not overwhelmed by the struggles of our world. He is heartbroken by it all. But he is not anxious or fearful or perplexed. He is our good and gracious God, and he is calling his children to step into the fray as never before.

Call me a fool. Call me naive. Call me unqualified to speak on such matters. You might be right. But of this I am sure: The Jesus answer is the answer.

FOR REFLECTION AND DISCUSSION

What tensions currently divide your community?

What would it look like for you to "bridge the gap" and promote reconciliation?

How is Jesus calling you to be an agent of peace?

What messy but necessary conversations do you need to have?

THE
REST
OF THE
DREAM

12

ANSWERED PRAYER

How the World Could Still Change

One afternoon, Robin and I were walking alone down into the Kidron Valley, shadowed by the Mount of Olives on one side and the remnants of the Temple Mount on the other. Emotions run high in that city where every step is weighted with wonder: *Did Jesus walk here? Gaze on that horizon? Climb that hill?* In many ways it is the land itself that pushes the story deeper into my thoughts. Structures come and go, paths are replaced by roads. But the steep hills and crooked valleys—these remain. These Jesus knew.

So there, in the valley between two storied hills, the two of us read one more time the story of our heart-heavy Savior on his way to Gethsemane. Was this the exact place? Probably not. Who knows? It doesn't matter. I'm close now—so is the wonder.

Jesus prayed for us here.

As we've learned, so much of that prayer comes down to that intimate, mysterious word: *one*. He prayed that we would be one. The mind reels—how important our unity was to him. And, often, how little it matters to us.

But that could change.

We've now spent several chapters and more than a few words describing this older-than-ancient love that stands at the center of all things. But the time for talk is soon past. Or as the apostle John implored: "Let us not love with word or speech but with actions and in truth."[1] Put another way, just talking about the genius of one isn't very smart at all. If we want things to change, we must now take action.

Two quick thoughts will help us:

1. We are on the same team. That's almost insultingly apparent, except . . .
2. We forget number 1.

TEEING OFF

One of our church sites is not far from a public golf course. One day a man, a new believer, was teeing off with someone who promptly turned around and faced in the opposite direction of the hole. I know all about overcompensating for a wayward tee shot. But this was different—nobody's slice is that bad. "What are you doing?" the new believer asked as his buddy took a big swing and knocked the ball far out of play.

"I hate that church."

As it turns out, he was taking aim at our building. Too far to hit it even by a long shot. But still, he made his point.

"But why would you hate that place?" asked the new believer. "Why would you do that?"

The wrong-way golfer proceeded to tell this man, who happens to be a friend of mine, that it was because some folks from his church had started attending The Crossing.

Batter up. Or better yet, *fore!*

Clearly this man was upset, but why? I can't pretend to know all that contributed to that moment. But it seems that at least part of his frustration was connected to where people attend church on any given Sunday. Now let me be clear: This is not a story about how we are growing and his church is not. I don't know that to be the case. The point of this story isn't even about poor little ol' us being the object of someone's nastiness. I'm embarrassed to admit I've been on the giving end of some nastiness myself. The real point is that a man who was enjoying his first few gulps of grace was taken aback by the actions of a friend who was opposing not the gospel but other Christians. Why?

Because that friend forgot we're on the same team.

Let's not kid ourselves. He is not the only forgetful follower. When our insecurities overtake our better judgment, we're quick to tee off against someone or some group whom we perceive to be a "threat." But a threat to what? We see some success or progress over "there" as a threat to what we're trying to accomplish for God over "here." The lofty ideal of "we're on the same team" is counterbalanced by the heavy desire to win. Whether it is a church, a ministry within a church, or a multinational organization, people make an investment and want a return. *I've given my life to this . . .* so naturally we want it to succeed.

There's nothing wrong with winning. I'm a big proponent

of it. So too is Paul. Later in Philippians he writes of *winning* the prize.[2] But must it be that you lose so that I can win? This does not sound very ingenious to me—that God would set up a sort of Kingdom Olympics where his children compete for a few prizes. Does that sound like God?

To be blunt, it sounds more like us. The thought running through many minds is not that we want another ministry to *lose*, but rather that they must *lose* so we might *win the prize. Let's face it,* some will quietly think, *there are only so many dollars and so many volunteers to go around.* Some will act as if there are only so many people in the world. This is, of course, technically true—on any given day there are a finite number of people on this planet and in our specific communities. But do any of us really think we'll run out of people to love, serve, and invite into the Kingdom?

Still, this oddness persists. And it is destructive.

A GAME WE CAN'T PLAY

In the mathematical world of game theory, we encounter the term *zero-sum game.* This is a game, a situation, an economy, where the end of the game always equals zero. A *plus one* always requires a *minus one,* for the game will always end in zero. It is a closed system wherein "each player gains what the other player loses."[3] When we perceive the Kingdom of God as a zero-sum game, we make all the wrong assumptions:

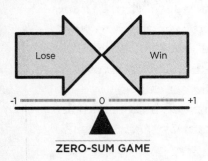

ZERO-SUM GAME

If people go to your church, mine won't grow.

If that donor gets involved with your work, we won't get funded.

If that person volunteers for your group, I won't have anyone.

If you win, I lose.

From here, it is a very short walk to being threatened by anyone else's success. And why not? "In such a game the two players have diametrically opposed interests."[4] Wrap it all with some good old-fashioned pride and now it's almost Darwinian. The Kingdom of God is really the survival of the fittest (or coolest, godliest, worthiest . . . you get the idea) ministry.

That can't be right.

God's plan does not fit in a mathematical game. And this approach does not reflect his love or genius. Note the visceral reaction you just had to the previous description. Nothing about that seems right when put in such stark terms. Even those who do not yet know Jesus bristle at the stunted thinking of such a simple equation. Deep down they long for something that transcends. A solution that will not fit on paper.

Now that seems right.

We are back to the selfless love that will, at the end of all time, defy all expectations. How will we now do more than talk about that love? How will the Kingdom take form before the eyes of our neighbors and friends? Let's go back to Paul's phrase "stand firm in one spirit,"[5] but then pause at this thought: We contend as one.[6]

"Striving together as one" is also how it is rendered. This phrase is translated from the verb *sunathleo*, which is really two words: *sun*, meaning "with," and *athleo*, meaning just what you think it means—"to compete in an athletic event." Paul describes the gospel being lived out in the arena as a team. Which makes us teammates. Which means (wait for it) . . . We're on the same team.

We may forget this from time to time, but that could change. It needs to change. Now. Not with a group hug—I promised you we wouldn't end things that way. We won't even end this book with an inspirational "go get 'em, team." The wounds gash too deep. The fear spreads too wide. The evil is too present and too greedy and too lightly taken by some. No, words won't be enough this time. Sappy emotion won't suffice. This is not the end of summer camp. Many in our world feel as though they are at the end of hope, so things need to change.

It is time for a revolution of sorts.

Be forewarned: This revolution might surprise us. We will not be able to control how it now plays out, for what will happen next (what is already happening) is Spirit breathed and Spirit driven. And Jesus told us we could no more control the Spirit than the wind.[7] So it will surprise us, this revolution.

It is intimate enough to fit in my heart and big enough to fill the whole world and then some. But the time for talk is soon over. The time for action is now. Everything we've considered in this book (and so much more) will now come into play.

Ready?

PAY ATTENTION TO THE SPACE BETWEEN

This is where the revolution could begin. We are on the same team, and as such share much in common—our Savior most of all. We have our differences, but we have been plunged into his redeeming sacrifice, and we are "all one in Christ Jesus."[8]

If we pull back for a wider view, we find some with whom we share even more. We tend to gather around some of those commonalities. This results in herds of various sizes and distinctions—from small groups and churches to denominations and global organizations.

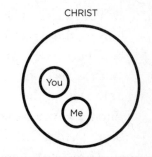

WE ARE ALL ONE IN CHRIST JESUS

We have rightly considered how individuals compose the many parts of the body of Christ. This is how those New Testament passages were written. And yet these larger groupings also have their own characteristics. Let's not use these precious last pages to discuss the history of denominations and the various midcourse corrections that have taken place throughout the years. But let's admit this much: We have been clumped into groupings for a multitude of reasons—some reasonable and some really awful. As early as the first century, Paul saw hints of what was to come, with people lining up behind him or Peter or Apollos.[9] His response: Christ is not divided, so cut it out.

And yet here we are with all these divisions and subdivisions. Can we ever reflect the genius of one? If the past two thousand years are any clue, some of this won't change until Jesus heals us fully. Does this mean we just live with our subdivided ways? No. Some of it must change now.

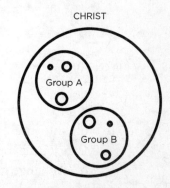

LARGER GROUPINGS OF THE
BODY OF CHRIST

For starters, *Christ is not divided, so cut it out.* We must face the sinful motivations from which some subgroups have been born. Such ugliness has no place in the body of Christ. The old divisions are gone, Paul told the Galatians. But what of the rest of these groups—large and small (shown here as A and B)? What of those who have coalesced around everything from doctrinal distinctions to personal preferences?

The starting point is the same throughout the illustration: Those *in Christ* are on the same team. We share in common all that we enjoy in Christ—grace, peace, hope, joy . . . and love, always love, for it is the greatest. Within the largest circle and all the smaller ones, we swim in the selfless love that is God.

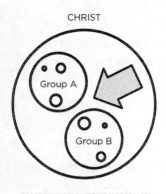

PAY ATTENTION TO THE SPACE BETWEEN

So we'll remember that: We are on the same team. But what can we do differently? How can we explore the brilliance of working together when we reside in different circles?

Pay attention to the space in between A and B.

This is the place from which exciting Kingdom endeavors will be born—when two groups get close enough to work in a space together. The notion is not new or unique to the Kingdom—we've already referenced collaborations of many kinds on these pages. It is built into the human story. It is how we flourish. One scholarly journal put it like this: "Some of the brightest ideas for social change grow in the spaces between organizations and sectors."[10] Let's say it again: The brightest ideas often grow *in the spaces between.*

This is where a new work can emerge. It is beyond the study of business schools and sociologists. For we have something that the corporations and institutions of the world do not—we are mysteriously connected by the person of Jesus, and the Creator will now bring into existence such good and lasting things. Parts of the body that barely said hello will now sense the Spirit rushing through, giving life to that which is outrageously, wonderfully different.

DEEPER RESOURCES

When two churches meet in this space, what's available for both will deepen. When a larger church brings its significant capital (human and financial) to a shared Kingdom space and then quietly refuses to allow the table to tilt their direction, their partner is honored—and often inspired. Selfless love has just lit the creative fuse. The smaller church can dream bigger, for they have more resources than ever before. When they in turn do not write off the big church as a "sellout," there is now mutual respect and a common goal. *Who cares who gets credit?* The smaller church now generously offers a better-informed idea than its partner could ever come up with. This is good stewardship for both churches, and the community is better served.

For too long we've watched one another from a distance, trying to come up with the next great thing on our own. Imagine what might happen if churches of all sizes—who have never worked together on anything—tried just one project together. What might come out of that space between them?

Unlikely Partners

The "you win/I lose" falsehood also thrives in the seam between churches and parachurch groups. This lie has set ministries on parallel tracks where the unspoken agreement is to stay out of each other's way. Deep down they're still competing. This must stop. Each must admit out loud old fears and tired rivalries and then, with God's help, set those things aside. An unlikely partnership can emerge as two groups face at least one challenge together.

Close enough to converse, these groups can now lob kind words into that space as they start taking action together. No more sentences starting with *If the church was doing its job* . . . or *If they actually went to church* . . . Instead, both "encourage . . . and build each other up."[11] I have a close friend who asks various parachurch organizations how often a local church cheers for their success. The consistent answer: *hardly ever.* Churches, pick up the phone. Reach out to those in your community doing good work. Encourage a fellow teammate.

Now, is the converse any better? How does a parachurch organization encourage involvement in a local church and celebrate what it does better than anyone else? If you're a leader in one such organization, meet with that church and ask them how you can be their advocate. This should be thought out and then lived out on both sides. And now that you've met, do something! There is room (and need, no doubt) in your community for that which has never been done before. So do something. Together. Don't worry who gets credit for what will soon happen. Such an approach is countercultural, but this is how the world will change again.

Fresh Ideas

The complications and challenges of this world will require bigger ideas, not rehashed versions of what we already think we know. To be surprised by God, we might need surprising thoughts. They will often come from these spaces.

Some of these new partnerships will involve parachurch organizations and other nonprofits working alongside one another in truly creative ways. We've already admitted it's easy for any of us to feel threatened when we start with the wrong assumptions. In the nonprofit sector, all the fears about limited resources in the face of heartbreaking realities come into play daily.

I'm humbled by the tireless work of people who bring relief and freedom to those who are not charity cases but image bearers of God. The dignity these workers show others, and the honor they express, is a lesson for the rest of us. I'm awed by their courage and challenged by their faith as they walk to the ragged edges of our world. For them, the soul-crushing burden of poverty is more than theory or even a well-told story. They know names. They are the ones who cry out like modern-day prophets against systemic evil that ravages a village, a people, a nation. When clean water can change a future, they see faces. Such organizations took action today. And tomorrow, they will do the same—all in the name of Jesus.

But these organizations have a chance to push back even more darkness. It will sound outrageous—to invest in something new when the urgent is so urgent. But bright ideas spark and glorious light come from the spaces between some of these organizations. Working together. Asking questions no one dared ask. Trying something that has no guarantee of circling back to an individual organization. Trusting that if it furthers the Kingdom, that is enough. (Though I happen to believe such open-handed ways leave those same hands open for much blessing from God in their work.) This is already happening in some ways, but so much more is possible. Many leaders mentioned on these pages share the rest of the dream.

One of these leaders is Mike Mantel, Living Water International's CEO. The idea of the many parts of Christ's church working together as one quickens his pulse. He dreams of creating new platforms for churches to work together. But here is his new thought: How can a global organization mobilize local churches toward their specific mission focus *even if it doesn't involve Living Water International*? Do you see what this means? The Kingdom is advanced and *another global organization might benefit more than his.* Such an endeavor is risky if we are playing a zero-sum game. But we are not. Are there other organizations that will join him in the "space between" to consider how—from our previous illustration—these larger circles might serve the smaller ones and each other? In so doing, the world is served.

This is but the beginning of a bright idea that will eventually shine light in a way not previously imagined. It is the catalyst for something new. It is not, however, a hopelessly naive invitation for all churches and organizations to disband so we can "just be the church together." Rather, let's be entrepreneurial in the spaces between us—each of us retaining our identity—and then see what happens. We are many parts. But we are one. Will something new form out of these spaces? Yes. It will be difficult, surprising, and liberating to acknowledge other ideas as they shape and change and even overtake our own. This is often the way to that new thing. And it is the way God intended us to create—together.

For the sake of the King and his Kingdom, it's time for our own *Braintrusts*.

In each of these scenarios and the countless possibilities not mentioned (there must be a Godzillion of them), the same truths hold: Refuse to invite much-needed life into your ministry and you will grow stale. Forget what it means to listen first and you will never be heard. Assume you are alone in this struggle and you will soon fade. Avoid the risk of collaboration and you'll miss some of God's best surprises.

Such is the wild frontier that is the space between A and B.

IT WILL ALWAYS BE PERSONAL

It is time to do something different, yes. Yet for all the talk of how churches and organizations can change (and they must), it is still people who compose the body of Christ. It is people, not faceless entities, who will love in deed and truth. The limit to our imagination may not be our distrust of God but of one another. The revolution will always ultimately begin when we dare to move closer and watch what God can do in the unlikeliest of spaces between people.

There are those, such as Gabe Lyons, founder of Q, who create the opportunities for surprising conversations that lead to unlikely partnerships—not just between organizations but principally between people. Some of us will now need to take an intentional step or two into such environments, where God might surprise us as we encounter fresh perspectives and discover new cohorts.

At other times, we'll experience God-ordained appointments we never saw coming. But in that shocking space between, the Spirit will breathe life. Like the weary Elijah, we are reminded there are others. A remnant, perhaps, not always an army. But it will be enough. For we are not alone. If we'll keep our eyes open and pay attention, God will speak to us in those spaces of new things.

For me once, it was the unlikely space between two pastors.

Nicky Gumbel is one of those forces of nature you really want to be around at least once in your life. Nicky is the founder of the Alpha Course, a course designed for non-believers to explore the truths of the gospel. He is also the vicar of Holy Trinity Brompton, a thriving church in London. The first time I met Nicky was through a mutual friend who thought we should know each other.

He graciously invited us to his home, and we stood in the kitchen—Robin and I with him and his lovely wife, Pippa. It was great. I was just thrilled to spend a little time with him and hear how God was working through this international ministry.

But then he asked us to come sit down for some tea. (It was London, after all.)

Over the course of the next couple of hours, Nicky asked me question after question about my ministry, my heart, and what I thought God was saying to me these days. Nicky was so graciously interested in our church. I was the one with all the questions, but I barely got them in.

And then Nicky spoke some of the most powerfully encouraging words directly into my soul. I didn't ask for it. I wasn't really sure what to do with it. It was a little overwhelming, what he said, and far too kind. But that heart-thumping, vision-stretching moment happened in the space between two fairly different pastors and two fairly different churches. I like to think an unlikely but lasting partnership was formed. In those spaces, the Spirit of God does surprising things. It wasn't to be the last time I was the recipient of Nicky and Pippa's hospitality and love. But on that first day, stumbling out into the brisk London air, I looked at my wife and said, "What just happened?"

She said to me, "God just spoke to you through that dear man. Pay attention."

When a barely teenaged boy came up to me recently and asked his pastor (that would be me), "How can I pray for you this week?" I could've politely dismissed it as a very nice thing, but I would've missed it. Instead, I gave him something specific to pray for me, and I believe he did just that. This is how the revolution begins. When unlikely moments happen in the spaces between.

So I paid attention.

When an older musician and a guitar player barely old enough to drive to rehearsal are on the same worship team at our church, there is a space between them. They can either hold back or lean in. When they lean in, something happens. The musician with many gigs under his belt doesn't dismiss the young upstart whose guitar keeps drifting out of tune. Instead, he patiently shows him a couple of things about stringing his instrument that no one had told him before. In that same space, later, in between services, it's the young prodigy who shows the wily veteran some new artists that he needs to be listening to. Inconsequential? I don't think so. Now both of their worlds are bigger. Pay attention.

When a guy with grease under his nails sits down with Mr. Buttoned Down, there is a space between them. When they talk about more than ESPN, pay attention. Something is happening. When they explore together some of the big hairy questions of Christianity in pursuit of Jesus, all of heaven is cheering them on.

When men and women gather at a children's hospital with a heartbroken family, there is a space between them. Few will know firsthand the pain of those parents. But when that group enters the room, they enter the chaos. They enter the space where no one wants to go. But it is here that the Spirit does a work that changes the world. Quiet tears. Full-throated sorrow. Open questions. Clinging to God and to one another. This is what grief laced with faith looks like. When months and years later those same people do what could not be first imagined—they laugh deeply—pay attention. God has begun to heal. This is a hope that does not disappoint, and the world is watching.

When you hear two women speak of their faith, this is good thing. When you listen closely and hear them share of their Muslim and Jewish backgrounds and the Jesus they now know and trust as Savior, pay attention. Such beauty does not fit in a headline. It defies politics and confounds experts. But in the space between them is something only God creates.

What he will do in these spaces cannot be predicted or engineered. But it can be noticed, celebrated, and even expected. It is life giving and light throwing and so very good. It is what we want. It is what we need. Your wisdom, their courage, her wisdom, his laughter, our life together . . . it is a gift for us. But it is the stuff of revolution.

The work of Andy Crouch again comes to mind. Looking at the early ripples of the Kingdom, he refers to "the 3, the 12, and the 120."[12] The smaller numbers—not the testimony of a mega-ministry—are how the world changed. In a later interview Crouch advises:

> The question to ask is, "Which group of three people has God put me with and what can we make together that will add something to culture that will reflect what God wants for culture— God's *shalom*, his peace?" And that's the only way it ever changes—when a small group of people create something.[13]

So what's keeping us from taking these steps? From trying these Kingdom experiments? What is it that's keeping us from joyous humility, better words, bigger hearts, and healthier cultures in our groups and churches? Perhaps we figure there's enough time to get to the soft stuff, the relationship stuff . . . later.

But is there time?

NOW, NOT LATER

Henry Cloud writes: "*Later* is one of the most abused drugs we have available to us. . . . It kind of makes [things] go away. Why? Because when we say it, we think we are actually *going* to do it 'later.'"[14]

Except we don't.

If the genius of one is truly that, then something gloriously unexpected awaits as we love differently. What starts as something intensely personal soon stretches further. Much further. This was the plan, and this was Jesus' prayer. *So that the world may know.*

We cannot wait until later. It will be too late.

Into a world splattered with hate, the body of Christ must now move—dripping with grace and veined with love.

We have that in common, this love that has always been. It is the costly, generous, healing, forgiving, won't-give-up love of God that chased us down. A love so extravagant and undeserved that we couldn't pay it back in a thousand lifetimes.

But we can share it. We can offer it. We can tell the story of that love by the way we now treat one another. And a world in desperate need will take notice.

It is time.

We aspens young and old, we many-colored threads in the tapestry, we many parts of one body . . . we really are better together. Collaborating. Submitting. Suffering. Listening. Serving. Encouraging. Forgiving. Championing. This is God's plan, and it is sheer genius. It is also the most powerful thing we can do in this world. To love as we have been loved. We do this and the words Jesus spoke to his Father on the worst night of his life come to life as an answered prayer.

FOR REFLECTION AND DISCUSSION

List some of your own sinful motivations that negatively affect your community. What would it look like to invite God to heal those parts of your life?

What are some unlikely partnerships that you can create?

What next step is God calling you to take?

How can you promote unity within your Christian community and work toward Jesus' prayer for oneness?

ACKNOWLEDGMENTS

As you watch someone give an acceptance speech at the Oscars, you immediately notice a sense of accomplishment coupled with the dread of forgetting to thank someone and the fear of going so long that the orchestra plays you into a commercial.

Writing the acknowledgments for a book is like giving an Oscars acceptance speech. And while I vow to keep this brief enough for the conductor to relax, I must write these words and soon say them aloud to so many—even at the terrifying risk of overlooking someone. For me, at this point, I am grateful for so many without whom there would be no sense of accomplishment. These are the people who reflect God's ingenious plan of working together as one.

First, thanks to my publisher, Don Pape, and his steadfast belief in this project. Thanks also to the rest of the team at NavPress and Tyndale—David Zimmerman, Helen Macdonald, and Caitlyn Carlson for making sense of my quirky stories and atypical narratives. David, your steady but easygoing hand was just what I needed.

To my agent, Mark Sweeney, for shepherding me through

this process. To Reggie McNeal for the first passionate push into the pool. To Pete Scazzero for blazing this trail and reminding our church we weren't crazy for caring about such things. To Dan Allender for leveraging the power of his good words toward my aching soul.

To my gifted friends and mentors: Chris Seay, Gabe Lyons, David Anderson, Mike Mantel, Mike Foster, Kenny Luck, Steve Haas, Amanda Bowman, Stan Patyrak, Linda Stanley, Dan Wolgemuth, Ted Vaughn, and Larry Osborne. I don't deserve it, but oh how you have encouraged me throughout the years:

To the intrepid (and slightly crazy) men who've traveled the world with me and been in most of these stories. Whether you're still here or serving elsewhere, you've made me a better man.

To our parents—Brooks and Jackie, Ann (and Bob): Thank you for creating the legacy of two loving families that in so many ways have become one.

To the rest: Ky and Terri, Chris and Tiffany, Jon and Karen, Rick and Janet. We may not be kids anymore or see one another as often as we like, but I carry your love in my heart and your fingerprints all over my life.

To a close circle that champions me in ways I could never repay: Rick and Kristi, Steve and Judy, John, Wiley, Dave, Andy, Randall, Dale, Anthony, Art, and Bill. You embody the humbling beauty of grace. You remind me again and again that I am not alone on this journey, nor would I ever want to be. Words fail me.

To the people of The Crossing: You allowed me to grow up and into my role as pastor over the years. Your honesty, passion, courage, and generosity make it safe for others to consider the way of Jesus. No matter where I go, there's no place like home.

To our cadre of young scholars: Thanks for letting me hang out with you. Matt, you make me think better and look way smarter than I really am. Ben, this book would simply not have come in on time without your tireless attention to detail. Thanks also for the questions at the end of the chapters.

To Donna, other people have mere assistants, but God gave me you. Thank you for bringing order to my chaos and gentleness to my day. You love me in a way that must make Jesus smile.

Lastly, to those three beautiful women—Robin, Alex, and Tori. I cannot express the profound joy it is to love each of you. Alex and Tori—my heart aches with the thought of being your dad. I am still hopelessly and utterly gobsmacked by you both. To your husbands, Michael and Jeremy, thank you for loving my daughters so well (next time you can join us with the sharks). To Robin, thank you for saying yes again and again to this grand adventure. For reasons I'll never fully understand, I get to laugh, cry, pray, dream, hope, and chase after God with you, my dear. What a gift.

I could go on, but I hear music.

NOTES

PROLOGUE
1. Clay Shirky, "From 'Why' to 'Why Not?'," *The Guardian*, May 17, 2009, https://www.theguardian.com/media/2009/may/18/internet-future.
2. Dean Williams, *Leadership for a Fractured World: How to Cross Boundaries, Build Bridges, and Lead Change* (Oakland, CA: Berrett-Koehler, 2015), 9.
3. David Kinnaman, *You Lost Me: Why Young Christians Are Leaving Church . . . And Rethinking Faith* (Grand Rapids, MI: Baker, 2011).
4. Rob Bell, "*Echad*," sermon delivered at Mars Hill Bible Church, Grand Rapids, Michigan, 2005.
5. John Ortberg, particularly his chapter "The Wonder of Oneness," in *Everybody's Normal Till You Get to Know Them* (Grand Rapids, MI: Zondervan, 2003).

CHAPTER 1: THE WORST NIGHT OF SOMEONE ELSE'S LIFE
1. Zechariah 9:9.
2. Mark 11:18.
3. For a scholarly discussion of where John 15–17 took place, see D. A. Carson, *The Gospel According to John* (Grand Rapids, MI: Eerdmans, 1990), 476–80.
4. John 14:31.
5. John 14:9, author's paraphrase.
6. John 17:10.
7. John 17:1.
8. John 17:5.
9. John 17:6.
10. Revelation 5:9, emphasis added.
11. John 17:20-23.

CHAPTER 2: WHEN SHARKS DANCE

1. Scot McKnight, *The Jesus Creed: Loving God, Loving Others* (Brewster, MA: Paraclete, 2004), 6. If you would like to gain a better appreciation of the Shema, McKnight's book is a good resource.
2. Rabbi Hayim Halevy Donin, *To Pray as a Jew: A Guide to the Prayer Book and the Synagogue Service* (New York: Basic Books, 1980), 144.
3. My faith (and yours) is more informed and thought-out because of such endeavors by theologians. To God be the glory for such men and women and their Scripture-soaked, highly educated brains.
4. John 8:56-59.
5. N. T. Wright, *Simply Christian: Why Christianity Makes Sense* (San Francisco: HarperCollins, 2006), 118.
6. John 1:3, *The Voice.*
7. Ezekiel 4:12, 15.
8. Ezekiel 37:17.
9. I am sure someone else has made this point and said this very thing. I'm trying to find someone to credit. ☺
10. Galatians 4:4.
11. 1 Corinthians 8:4-6.
12. Christopher Wright, *The Mission of God: Unlocking the Bible's Grand Narrative* (Downers Grove, IL: InterVarsity, 2006), 111.
13. 1 John 4:8.
14. Scot McKnight, *One.Life: Jesus Calls, We Follow* (Grand Rapids, MI: Zondervan, 2010), 150.
15. John 17:21.

CHAPTER 3: SHEER GENIUS

1. Proverbs 3:19.
2. Romans 12:4-5.
3. Michael C. Grant, "The Trembling Giant," *Discover*, October 1, 1993.
4. Leonard Matheson, *Your Faithful Brain: Designed for So Much More!* (Bloomington, IN: WestBow, 2014), 164–65.
5. Psalm 139:13-14.
6. Psalm 139:15.
7. F. Brown, S. Driver, and C. Briggs, *The Brown-Driver-Briggs Hebrew and English Lexicon* (Peabody, MA: Hendrickson, 2005), 955.

CHAPTER 4: KEEP ONE EYE ON THE FISH, THE OTHER ON THE BEAR

1. Terry Eagleton, quoted in Andy Crouch, *Culture Making: Recovering Our Creative Calling* (Downers Grove, IL: InterVarsity, 2008), 10. This will not be the only reference to this seminal work by Crouch. The ground

he covers is different from the focus of this book. But his thoughts about culture and the opportunities for Christians in our world are essential. Read it. Do something with it. You're welcome.

2. *Merriam Webster's Essential Learner's English Dictionary*, s.v. "culture."
3. Crouch, *Culture Making*, 19. Told you I'd mention this book again.
4. Edgar Schein, "The Concept of Organizational Culture: Why Bother?," *Classics of Organization Theory*, edited by Jay Shafritz and J. Steven Ott (Independence, KY: Cengage Learning, 2011), 355.
5. Matthew 28:19-20.
6. Schein, *Classics of Organization Theory*, 354.
7. Philippians 2:2.
8. Walter Bauer, *A Greek-English Lexicon of the New Testament and Other Early Christian Literature*, revised and edited by Frederick William Danker (Chicago: University of Chicago Press, 1979), 1065.
9. Philippians 2:1 (emphasis added).
10. Peter Scazzero, *The Emotionally Healthy Leader: How Transforming Your Inner Life Will Deeply Transform Your Church, Team, and the World* (Grand Rapids, MI: Zondervan, 2015), 56.
11. 1 Peter 5:8.

CHAPTER 5: A STORY ABOUT GUNS

1. Romans 12:3.
2. Philippians 2:3.
3. Ortberg, *Everybody's Normal*, 38.
4. Cornelius Plantinga, *Engaging God's World: A Christian Vision of Faith, Learning, and Living* (Grand Rapids, MI: Eerdmans, 2002), 20.
5. Philippians 2:5.
6. Scazzero, *Emotionally Healthy Leader*, 55.
7. Bauer, *Greek-English Lexicon*, 986.
8. Steven D. Levitt and Stephen J. Dubner, *Think Like a Freak: The Authors of Freakonomics Offer to Retain Your Brain* (New York: William Morrow, 2014), 19–20.
9. Michael P. Nichols, *The Lost Art of Listening: How Learning to Listen Can Improve Relationships*, 2nd ed. (New York: Guilford Press, 2009), 144.
10. 1 Timothy 1:14.
11. Timothy Keller, *The Reason for God: Belief in an Age of Skepticism* (New York: Dutton, 2008), 181.
12. Ibid., 181.
13. See F. F. Bruce, *Philippians*, New International Critical Commentary (Peabody, MA: Hendrickson, 1989); and Michael J. Gorman, *Apostle of the Crucified Lord: A Theological Introduction to Paul and His Letters* (Grand Rapids, MI: Eerdmans, 2004).

CHAPTER 6: AT SOME POINT ALL OF OUR MOVIES STINK

1. F. P. Leverett, ed., *A New and Copious Lexicon of the Latin Language* (Philadelphia: J. B. Lippincott, 1896).
2. Ecclesiastes 4:9.
3. Ed Catmull and Amy Wallace, *Creativity, Inc.: Overcoming the Unseen Forces That Stand in the Way of True Inspiration* (New York: Random House, 2014).
4. Ibid., 86.
5. Ibid.
6. Roger von Oech, *A Whack on the Side of the Head: How You Can Be More Creative*, as quoted in Nancy Beach, *An Hour on Sunday: Creating Moments of Wonder and Transformation* (Grand Rapids, MI: Zondervan, 2004), 178.
7. Catmull and Wallace, *Creativity, Inc.*, 90. Emphasis in original.
8. Hebrews 10:24.
9. Bauer, *Greek-English Lexicon*, 780.
10. Ibid.
11. Hebrews 10:25.
12. Catmull and Wallace, *Creativity, Inc.*, 92.

CHAPTER 7: THE DISCLAIMER

1. Rob Cross, Reb Rebele, and Adam Grant, "Collaborative Overload," *Harvard Business Review* (January–February 2016), accessed March 28, 2017, https://hbr.org/2016/01/collaborative-overload.
2. Ibid.
3. Ibid.
4. Catmull and Wallace, *Creativity, Inc.*, 86.
5. Cross, Rebele, and Grant, "Collaborative Overload."
6. Ibid.
7. Henry Cloud, *Necessary Endings: The Employees, Businesses, and Relationships That All of Us Have to Give Up in Order to Move Forward* (New York: HarperBusiness, 2011), 7.
8. 1 Corinthians 12:21.
9. 1 Corinthians 12:18.

CHAPTER 8: LIFE AND DEATH

1. Rodney Stark's *Victory of Reason: How Christianity Led to Freedom, Capitalism, and Western Success* (New York: Random House, 2006) is a great place to start. The writings and talks of Chuck Colson (see *The Faith: What Christians Believe, Why They Believe It, and Why It Matters* [Grand Rapids, MI: Zondervan, 2008]) also give intellectual heft to the claim that good has been advanced by the people of God.

2. ESV.
3. Brown, Driver, and Briggs, *Brown-Driver-Briggs Hebrew and English Lexicon*, 615.
4. NLT.
5. Matthew 23:26.
6. James 1:19.
7. John Ortberg, *Now What?: God's Guide to Life for Graduates* (Grand Rapids, MI: Zondervan, 2011).
8. Dietrich Bonhoeffer, *Life Together: A Discussion of Christian Fellowship* (New York: Harper and Row, 1954), 97–98.
9. Martin Buber, *I and Thou* (New York: Touchstone, 1996), 12.
10. Ortberg, *Everybody's Normal Till You Get to Know Them*, chapter 7.
11. Matthew 18:15.
12. Romans 12:18.

CHAPTER 9: THE COLOR OF A COBRA'S EYES

1. Proverbs 20:19.
2. 1 Timothy 5:13. Translation is from Bauer, *Greek-English Lexicon*, 800.
3. Romans 1:29-30.
4. Bauer, *Greek-English Lexicon*, 1098.
5. Genesis 16:13.
6. The first time I heard this word was in Jonah Goldberg, "Schadenfreudtastic," *The National Review*, September 30, 2011, http://www.nationalreview.com/corner/278819/schadenfreudtastic-jonah-goldberg.

CHAPTER 10: HANG ON TO THAT RED SHIRT

1. 2 Corinthians 1:3-4.
2. Translation is from Bauer, *Greek-English Lexicon*, 457.
3. Horatio G. Spafford, "It Is Well with My Soul," public domain.
4. Bauer, *Greek-English Lexicon*, 502, 757.
5. Dallas Willard, *The Allure of Gentleness: Defending the Faith in the Manner of Jesus* (San Francisco: HarperOne, 2015), 160. Emphasis in original.
6. Ben Patterson, *Waiting: Finding Hope When God Seems Silent* (Downers Grove, IL: InterVarsity, 1989), 164.
7. John 20:29.
8. J. I. Packer, *Knowing God* (Downers Grove, IL: InterVarsity, 1993), 53. As quoted by Matt Perman, "How Can Jesus Be God and Man?" *Desiring God*, October 5, 2006, http://www.desiringgod.org/articles/how-can-jesus-be-god-and-man.
9. John 1:14, MSG.
10. John 20:21.

11. Augustine, quoted in *Catechism of the Catholic Church* (London: Burns & Oates, 1999), 435.
12. Reggie McNeal, *Missional Renaissance: Changing the Scorecard for the Church* (San Francisco, CA: Jossey-Bass, 2009), 24.
13. 2 Corinthians 4:11.
14. John Piper, "His Body: The Fullness of Him Who Fills All in All," *Desiring God*, September 20, 1992, http://www.desiringgod.org /messages/his-body-the-fullness-of-him-who-fills-all-in-all.
15. Michael Gerson, "The Children among Syria's Ruins," *Washington Post*, October 15, 2015, https://www.washingtonpost.com/opinions /syrian-children-among-the-ruins/2015/10/15/8d0510de -7360-11e5-8d93-0af317ed58c9_story.html?utm_term =.927ab60a4f99.
16. Ibid.
17. Philippians 4:6.
18. 2 Corinthians 1:3-4.

CHAPTER 11: THE JESUS ANSWER

1. Stephen Collinson, "Who Can Heal America?" *CNN*, July 9, 2016, http://www.cnn.com/2016/07/08/politics/dallas-heal-america-obama -clinton-trump/.
2. Ibid.
3. John Inazu, *Confident Pluralism: Surviving and Thriving through Deep Difference* (Chicago: University of Chicago Press, 2016).
4. David Kinnaman and Gabe Lyons, *Good Faith: Being a Christian When Society Thinks You're Irrelevant and Extreme* (Grand Rapids, MI: Baker, 2016), 106.
5. Edwin Friedman, *A Failure of Nerve: Leadership in the Age of the Quick Fix* (New York: Church Publishing, 2007), 58.
6. Ibid.
7. Murray Bowen, cited in Friedman, *A Failure of Nerve*, 55–56.
8. John 3:19-20.
9. McKnight, *Jesus Creed*, 33.
10. Ibid., 37.
11. Friedman, *A Failure of Nerve*, 62.
12. Ibid., 84.
13. Proverbs 15:1.
14. Friedman, *Failure of Nerve*, 68.
15. David French, "America Is Driving toward the Abyss, and It's Time We Hit the Brakes," *National Review*, July 8, 2016, http://www .nationalreview.com/article/437625/dallas-police-shooting-demands -calm-debate.

16. David Anderson, *Gracism: The Art of Inclusion* (Downers Grove, IL: InterVarsity Press, 2007), 159.

17. To see those photos, see "Ferguson Awaits Grand Jury Decision," CBS, November 19, 2014, http://www.cbsnews.com/videos/ferguson-awaits -grand-jury-decision/.

18. This is a variation on a scenario suggested by Friedman, *Failure of Nerve*, 58.

19. David Anderson, *I Forgrace You: Doing Good to Those Who Have Hurt You* (Downers Grove, IL: InterVarsity, 2011), 37.

20. John Paul Lederach, *The Moral Imagination: The Art and Soul of Building Peace* (New York: Oxford University Press, 2005), 175.

21. Galatians 6:9.

22. Psalm 34:14.

23. Keller, *Reason for God*, 188–89.

24. Lederach, *The Moral Imagination*, 18.

CHAPTER 12: ANSWERED PRAYER

1. 1 John 3:18.

2. Philippians 3:14.

3. Michael Maschler, Eilon Solan, and Shmuel Zamir, *Game Theory* (New York: Cambridge University Press, 2013), 111.

4. Ibid.

5. Philippians 1:27.

6. Philippians 1:27. Translation from Bauer, *Greek-English Lexicon*, 964.

7. John 3:8.

8. Galatians 3:28.

9. 1 Corinthians 1:12.

10. Satish Nambisan, "Platforms for Collaboration," *Stanford Social Innovation Review*, Summer 2009, accessed March 29, 2017, https://ssir.org/articles/entry/platforms_for_collaboration.

11. 1 Thessalonians 5:11.

12. Crouch, *Culture Making*, 240.

13. Andy Crouch, "Being Culture Makers," interview with StudentSoul.org, January 2007, accessed March 29, 2017, http://andy-crouch.com/articles /being_culture_makers.

14. Cloud, *Necessary Endings*, 181.